Have you ever thought what it might be like to visit all the away grounds in the Isthmian League South East league in one season? Have you ever wanted to give up Saturdays and Tuesday evenings, whatever the weather, whatever the distance to support your team in the 8th tier of English football? Thought not, however there are those that do. Following Ashford United (The Nuts and Bolts) during the 2024/25 season this is how it went for four men in a car.

10/8/24. Erith Town.
17/8/24. Harrow Borough.
26/8/24. Sittingbourne.
7/9/24. Deal Town.
10/9/24. Ramsgate.
24/9/24. Cray Valley PM.
28/9/24. Chertsey Town.
15/10/24. East Grinstead Town.
19/10/24. Eastbourne Town.
26/10/24. Lewes.
2/11/24. Burgess Hill Town.
9/11/24. Lancing.
23/11/24. Beckenham Town.
26/11/24. Deal Town.
30/11/24. Merstham.
14/12/24. Sheppey United.
26/12/24. Hythe Town.
4/1/25. Steyning Town.
18/1/25. Sevenoaks Town.
1/2/25. Herne Bay.
15/2/25. Broadbridge Heath.
1/3/25. AFC Croydon Athletic.
22/3/25. Phoenix Sports.
5/4/25. Three Bridges.
18/4/25. Littlehampton Town.
26/4/25. Margate.

PRE SEASON

It seems only a few weeks since our last trip away (end of April down in Lancing and yes we lost 4 2). Back then the talk in the car was all about who might be staying for next season, who might the new manager bring in and who will be the new manager anyway? We soon got to hear of Danny Kedwell's appointment and quickly after that came the new signings; Craig Stone, James Dunne, Will Moses, Louis Collins, Dean Beckwith, Gary Lockyer, Mikey Berry, Jack Saunders, Joey Taylor, Mitchell Beeney and Lee Martin. So they are serious!

We start off with 3 comfortable home games that probably didn't test us in truth but wow we look good. The first away day for the tourists was the familier Hollands and Blair, the scene of our FA cup triumph last season. A nice little ground near Gillingham and they're always welcoming there; no overcharging at the gate and the pitch is excellent. Good catering and a nice club. There are a few away supporters there doing their best to make a bit of noise to encourage the new team but for whatever reason we don't fire in the first half and find ourselves, probably against the run of play, 2 nil down at half time! The H&B team seem very up for the fight and Mikey Berry's debut is often punctuated with him being flattened by somewhat over zealous preseason challenges. He looks like a real talent though (another one!) and keeps jumping back to his feet. The other new talent and (at time of writing still a trialist) is not only an extremely exciting winger but also has the coolest name in the dressing room; Marley St Louis. His runs down the wing and the general upping in our game looks like we'll not only equalise but win this one. In the end we only got one back but there was enough there to give the tourists belief for the coming season.

After home defeat to Folkestone we all knew in the car that Dartford would be a tricky test. A warm day, the first game this pre season on grass and against a team relegated from the National League South last season and desperate to go back up again. The first of a two game weekend as well (another home game against Kennington tomorrow) and we're obviously making the most of our opportunities to build and gel as a team. Some criticise The Princes Park Stadium but us tourists liked the place; modern wrap around ground, lovely grass pitch, good and clear PA and the acoustics meant the 'Ashford few' were able to make some noise and really got behind the lads and that was easy given their considerable effort on the pitch. Only downside was the entry cost for a pre season friendly which caused audible heavy sighs at the turnstile!

Honestly we're knocking the ball about like we're the Isthmian Premier side and Jack Saunders and Mikey Berry link really well in midfield and are great to watch. Dunne has to play at right back with several away on holiday and does really well. We have Alex Breffo playing at the back as well as a trialist and he certainly looks the part. Half time and somehow they scored twice against the run of play and despite Gary Lockyer hitting the bar with a free kick and Max Walsh heading just over from an excellent Lee Martin cross, we find ourselves down but by no means disheartened.

The second half is a repeat of the first and if anything we look even more threatening. Marley has his own song and that's the first time us tourists can remember a trialist having his own song but he's well worth it and again is an inspiration not just for his attacking skills but his hard work tracking back as well. We manage to score a lovely goal, Martin to Walsh, lovely cross and tap in for Noah. There's a purr behind the goal followed by much singing. Let's forget the goal they scored as well and the 3 1 final score line shall we; could have won that one. Just need to create a few more chances in the final third probably but Danny will sort that out.

A Dartford security guard comes up to us after the game to tell us how impressed he was with AUFC and reckons we have the makings of a really good side. We weren't going to argue and went home with smiles on our faces with discussion about what was for dinner not getting going

ntil close to Ashford. We always travel in hope but in recent seasons, limited expectations. We
on't want to get carried away as we know how tough this season will be. We try to agree on
avourites for promotion and can't. The list, from this car anyway, included Margate,
ittingbourne, Ramsgate, Deal, Croydon and Herne Bay. As long as we compete, play good
ootball and get the crowds in making a noise then we'll be happy. COYNAB!

/ALTHAMSTOW AND ERITH TOWN

fter a better than expected journey Walthamstow was chaotic with a number of Youth games
ad just finished and a constant stream of parents cars did their best to block the narrow
ntrance to the ground.

here was even more confusion with our players and management milling around as we had
een advised that the main pitch and changing rooms were unavailable as there was a SCEFL
vel game kicking off at 3pm! The game was canceled and messages posted. 10 Minutes later
owever as both teams were there it was agreed to play a game on the adjacent 3G training
tch surrounded by a high mesh fence.

Not ideal by any means but it would give the lads a runout.

To add to this there was no seating, covered areas as it was a hot day, tea or bar facilities but fans were still charged £5 to watch the game peering through a mesh fence.

Despite the on/off/on scenario a reasonable smattering of AUFC fans were in attendance in the gate of 49!

We're the better side getting into a good rhythm and playing some neat passing football but the ref's given a penalty for what looked like a good tackle! One down then! We're pressing and soon get on level terms. Noah wins the ball on the right and the perfect square ball for Max. 1-1 at Half time.

ame vein second half until but there's a mass altercation and everyone seems to be joining in. ll very silly and we don't need this in a 'friendly'. Less said the better.

ventually we get going again and Louis hits a fine strike into the top corner. Max hits the rossbar but Walthamstow came back and score twice in the last 8 minutes with former Ashford layer Kymani Thomas setting up their winner with the literally the last kick of the game. hat seemed a tad unfair. Everyone kisses and makes up at the end with handshakes all ound.

ll in all a bizarre day and next an FA Cup home game and then the serious business of the ague away at Erith.

e head to the Stanmore Stadium in Thamesmead; home of the newly promoted Erith town nd a much better place to watch football than where they were playing a couple of years ago.

lovely summers day and a grass pitch although the 6 yard box at one end looks like a kids and pit and we hope nobody gets hurt as a result.

What followed was an incredible game for the first match of this year's league campaign. Following our comfortable home win in the cup last week we're all upbeat and there are some wildly optimistic predictions among the tourists. Somehow, however, we find ourselves 2 nil down at half time and against the run of play. There's still hope as a few sample the barbecue at half time (£5 and 'OK' according to our gastronomic expert);

The second half gets going and it's all Ashford but the ball just won't go in! It looks like it's going to be one of those days as we're still down and 70 minutes have gone. Noah's goal gives us hope then substitute Max Walsh scrambles hope and we're level. Mad scenes behind the goal and when Noah hits the post heads are in hands but 10 seconds later Gary meets a cross with a diving header and we're in the lead and it's pandemonium!

Best to watch the highlights on Nuts and Bolts TV YouTube channel but amazing scenes. How we then didn't manage the match out is best not talked about but for them to equalise in the 97th minute certainly changed the mood. A draw is a point and at halftime we'd have taken that. They seem well happy and they celebrate a gate of 174 (half from Ashford probably!).

Driving home we're delighted we were there and hope that the game inspires more to come on the coach to Harrow Borough in the FA Cup.

HARROW BOROUGH

's been a while since there's been talk of a coach for fans to an away game however it's a ing again! Having apparently received several requests and expressions of interest in a coach r the Harrow Borough game in the FA Cup the new management sprung into life to see what uld be done. After lots of behind the scenes work from the new owners and with quotes tained here, there and everywhere, Ian Scammell managed to get a reasonable quote from ayliss Coaches and Ernie Warren kindly stepped up to make the arrangements. So we find rselves at the Homelands on a beautiful summer's day awaiting our ride to North London. Are e leaving early enough time? Are we going clockwise or anti clockwise around the M25? Shall e just leave it to the professionals to get us there before kick off!?

Like most tours the talk, initially at least, centres around who people think should be in the starting 11 and who should be on the bench. With so much individual talent available we agree that none of us would like to be Danny Kedwell having to make the decision of who to play today; too difficult. There have been signs recently that things are beginning to click but it's one game at a time and Harrow Borough are an unknown entity. It's a long, long drive into the unknown however we miraculously make it past the accursed A3 roadworks on the M25 and find ourselves at the somewhat run down Roger's Family Stadium in Harrow. We've no idea how the bus will turn around or park even but again we'll leave it to the driver who knows what he's doing. The elderly guys on the turnstiles seem a bit shocked to see a bus load of Nuts and Bolts supporters approach and we're told that they don't normally have people turning up to watch their games; tongue in cheek but it's strange so few are there and Ashford fans seem more numerous in numbers than the Harrow support with other Nuts and Bolts finding their way there on train or car; good to see and to be part of.

13

s a hot day and there is no cover behind the goals. There's a bar away from the ground and
side the facilities are basic. A very friendly lady does her best to provide the basics (drinks,
urgers, chips etc) with a smile but our testers find the chips a bit greasy and overpriced and
eirdly there are no bins around the place for the rubbish. The PA is basic and just about
udible (We're hoping ours is better soon!) and we've been to better places in all honesty.

s a grass pitch with several slopes but playable and a full squad is there warming up when we
rive. Danny Kedwell seems upbeat, relieved and delighted that all the players and the fans
ave made it.
opes are high as the first half kicks off however we seem to struggle. They attack down the left
veral times and we pick up a couple of yellow cards with robust tackles; we can't argue. We
an't seem to get our rhythm although there are passages of good possession. We don't seem
 be able to create much in all honesty and we're relieved to get to half time all square. Danny
ll sort them out at the break so we become more of a threat in the second half.

It's not getting much better after the restart but they miss their chances and Marley manages a superb goal line clearance t keep things all square; maybe it is our day after all! Perhaps not, they score and to be honest deserve their lead. We get going and Max is making a difference down the left and Lee is playing in a more effective forward role but we still don't seem to be able to create a clear cut chance. The excellent Jack Saunders at last finds an excellent cross, our first real chance and it falls to Gary Lockyer who heads home to much rejoicing and maybe we can go on to win this after all. A late header is brilliantly saved by their keeper and the ref inexplicably decides it's a goal kick and not a corner; maybe a draw is going to be a decent result today. As the final whistle blows we stand and applaud the effort all the Ashford players put in today. We didn't make things happen in the final third at all today but the draw today means a replay on Tuesday; "we'll win that" Danny says after the game.

Most are exhausted on the coach and the traffic, whilst heavy, doesn't get in the way of a reasonable trip home. We agree among ourselves that next week and the next 3 games in particular will tell us a lot about the team we support and how far we've come, how patient we need to be and what realistic expectations we should have. There's a digger in the car park when we get back to the Homelands; could this be work on the new car park?

The new owners have facilitated today's coach and want success desperately and clearly know the fans are vital if the club's to grow. Us tourists feel valued and appreciated so lets hope there are more of these coach trips going forward although we'll probably be back in the car for the next away game which is more local. Won't it be nice to one day be counting how many coaches we'll be needing as opposed to asking whether we have enough fans to fill a coach; one day!

SITTINGBOURNE

After an exciting Friday night back at the Homelands against a strong Margate side, under the lights (eventually!) we're quickly back in action on August Bank Holiday Monday away at Sittingbourne. Our opponents are tipped by many for promotion this season however they lost on Saturday away at Ramsgate so will that make them a wounded beast today and more dangerous or will they be vulnerable? We're about to find out!

It's the usual cross country drive for a 1 O'clock kick off at their ground very 'out of town' and near the science park. It seems a shame that a good club like the Brickies don't have a better stadium like the one they used to play at and we just hope the pitch behaves itself this time for a change. The narrow road winds it's way up onto the Downs and we get there just in time for one passenger who is feeling increasingly car sick in the back. There's nowhere to park until an eagle eyed fan in the car park sees someone leaving and relax, we've arrived and can park on a beautiful summers day. We're warmly welcomed at the gate and there's no escaping the programme salesman. The place looks better than the last few times (probably the weather and the early season pitch) but we all know this has not been a happy hunting ground over the years. There's a new 'Blakeys Shed' at one end we see; small but will do the job for their hardcore loyal support.

Lots of Ashford fans here as usual and we try to make some noise to support the team. As we make our way behind the goal it's a surprise that there are no stewards in sight given Sittingbourne fans don't change ends. Fortunately there are no hot heads looking for trouble and the match kicks off in the sunshine without incident. Our team always looks strong but Noah is out injured and Tolu and Jack Saunders are back in the lineup.

Unfortunately the first half isn't an exciting watch with both teams trying to win a hard fought midfield battle. The excellent James Dunne gets a booking as does Gary who's looking a bit frustrated with things. Louis Collins never stops running and deservedly makes his own goal charging down their keeper and we're ahead at half time. A professional job so far but can we keep it up in the heat?

At half time obviously we swap ends and hearts sink as we see the Sombrero Man who spends his time trying to wind up away fans every time we visit. How haven't they dealt with this bloke before he causes real trouble? We tell a steward that he's standing next to a sign that actually says 'no standing in this area' and she just shrugs and does nothing. Later another steward comes along and again fans point out he's standing where he shouldn't, getting in the way of seated supporters and this steward just stands with him for 10 minutes again doing nothing. One day he's going to cause serious problems and Sittingbourne FC can't say they haven't been warned.

Sadly, the game itself goes downhill for us and we concede a really poor equaliser. The next two goals give us a sinking feeling and it's obvious there's not going to be a fight back today. There is a synchipatic relationship between a team and it's fans and whilst there are efforts to make some noise and cheer the lads on today it's muted. Unfortunately there's little to cheer today and it's probably a game best forgotten. Danny will have learnt lots from this but the reality is we're second best by some distance today.

It's a bit of a trudge back to the car and a thoroughly depressing Bank Holiday Monday for us. It's strange how a simple game can get to you and the mood swings are ridiculous. We wonder if we'll pass the speeding motorist on the way back who looked like he damaged his tyre swerving to avoid us on the way and (having taken an even more circuitous back country road route) we don't. We all agree that a bounce back in the cup on Saturday is now very much needed and we think we'll beat Three Bridges well. It's a long season and we've had a slow start but when we get on a roll why can't we get the sort of gates Deal got today against Ramsgate (nearly 2000). We all still believe in the car but there's no denying we're downbeat today. Once we've beaten Three Bridges we have Ramsgate in the League and Deal in a cup game so maybe someone walked under a ladder before the fixtures were drawn this season; it a very tough start but we have an excellent squad and once we get going we'll be fine. COYNAB.

DEAL

After the 6 1 thumping of Three Bridges last weekend it seems too long a gap before our next game (especially with last Tuesday's game postponed). The players should be fresh enough fo the Deal encounter in the FA Trophy and the majority in our car anyway don't think Lee Martin will be missed too much. What went on there? The club put out a statement and we all agree that whilst you have to respect his pedigree etc he hadn't really done much for us in the short time he was at the Homelands. Who knows what really goes on with players and it's probably lazy thinking to assume it's all down to money.

There's a disturbing conversation in the car on the way (often the way with middle aged men freed from real life for the afternoon) and this chat starts off discussing the pros and cons of NHS poo tests on men of a certain age to how much demand there is for a book written by an AUFC supporter. This author and supporter (who will remain unnamed) is a close buddy of on urist in our car (maybe two actually) and has written a book detailing the final resting places of x Surrey Cricketers; yes seriously! It's obviously going to be a best seller and should be tocked in the new club shop for Christmas. This inane chat, whilst not untypical, is probably overing pre match nerves. Although we're grown adults, we are AUFC fans and take upporting the team probably far too seriously than is healthy and we know Deal will be a hard eam to beat; oh and will we be able to park? We're ridiculously early again so there's loads of pace to park.

ore important is today's game and progressing in another cup. We all respect Deal for what ey've achieved in the last year or so and their recent crowd against Ramsgate (approaching 000) was some going. They're going to be hard to beat today and it's on grass (should we stop sing grass pitches as an excuse when things don't go well?). Coach Paul Murray's son Macca their skipper as well so does that mean we'll get insider info? All will be revealed and for ome of us this is a first venture to Deal Town FC and we tourists always like a new ground.

s not too bad a ground; 3 or 4 places to get refreshments, cover here and there and they're oviously trying to maximise what they've got. A pulled pork and chips dish is ravenously onsumed by a fan behind the goal, costs £7 and gets the thumbs up. A pint is apparently £4.50 o London prices have not yet reached Deal. They even have a rather smart electronic coreboard and we wonder whether we'll get something new like this soon?

decent crowd watch the two sides go into battle and it is a bit of a battle in the first half with ry few clear cut chances and little to report. We reckon we edged it on points but there's not uch in it to be honest. Does this go straight to penalties or is there extra time if it ends like this? Everyone is wondering and we all know there won't be a replay. Please let the second half be better. As the second half goes on we're the better side and there are some strong performances all over the pitch; Marley, Tolu, Stone and Dunne are particularly impressing and it's the skipper who deservedly puts us ahead from close range and look at the smile on his face:

We hang on and we use the bench which means Lanre Azeez is back however very sadly he picks up what looks like another bad injury. We don't know if it's the same injury or a new knee problem but it's such bad luck for a lad who spent several weeks trying to overcome a pre-season injury. Let's hope it's not as bad as it looked. Danny puts in a short shift off the bench and is looking fitter than a few weeks ago and we hold out to win with few scares. Another cup run then; this is fun!

A happy car on the drive home however there is concern that the Tuesday game sees us against Ramsgate already. We all agree that we'd have preferred to be playing them a few months into the season when the team has really gelled. There will be two or three new players incoming we understand and maybe one on Tuesday. There's much speculation but we have no clue really who it could be and it's all part of the football supporter soap opera.

RAMSGATE

It always seems a long drive for some reason and tonight with the road to Faversham and the Thanet Way shut it feels even worse. In the wind and rain however we manage to navigate the small country roads and eventually make it to their ground in the middle of built up Ramsgate. Why was this game scheduled for a Tuesday night? Were it a Saturday there would be a big crowd and lots of noise instead people are huddled in what shelter they can find and there's not much of an atmosphere which is unusual. The ground here is strange in that there never looks to be that many here but because it's a big, old fashioned site the crowds are often more than you'd think and in the end there are over 600 here.

here are a couple of new faces warming up but nobody knows their names. At last the Team eup is discovered and we have William Duprey (ex Haringey Borough Google tells us) starting d Theo Osinfolarin (wasn't he at Herne Bay last season?) on the bench. Nobody pays much tention to the Ramsgate team as we know they'll have quality throughout but Ashford old boy om Carlse is on the bench and says hello as we walk past.

uis Collins is all over them in the first half and they're clearly scared of his pace. In fact we're ging this and it's encouraging to see so many of our guys playing well. They are a very good de as we know and they take their first real chance although was there an offside in the build ? The match highlights might show that and also clear up whether or not the excellent Mikey rry deserved a yellow card for simulation when, to us, he was brought down going into the x. Mikey is all over the pitch, working so hard and his excellent shot brings out a fingertip ve from their keeper meaning we head into the break a goal down. We're still in it and we're rtainly as good as them.

couple of quick set piece goals straight after the break kill us. We're still fighting however and ads aren't dropping which is good to see. Mikey Berry is clearly brought down in the penalty x but for reasons best known to the ref a free kick is awarded outside the box (again the highlights should clear that one up!). The weather worsens and rain sweeps across the ground apposite for the atmosphere behind the goal. It's a bit miserable to be honest. Jo Taylor scores his usual goal and we're four behind but to our credit keep going and have a couple of chances of our own.

The long trudge home is pretty quiet in the car. Usual platitudes are exchanged and there's a b of laughter about a doom and gloom comment on the socials by someone clearly not at the game. The reality is this game probably came too early for this new group of players. It should be closer when we play the return fixture in November and we're all confident that we'll be OK and will have a good season. We will only have two points from four games for most of September and the league table won't look pretty for a while however there's no sense of pani amongst us tourists and nights like tonight will soon be forgotten especially if, as expected, we bounce back hard on Saturday in the FA Cup against Corinthian. Horrible night in Ramsgate b we're all still very excited about Saturday and hope there'll be lots of support, lots of noise and lots of goals in the Corinthian net. Gary's 100th appearance for AUFC if he's selected; he usually likes an occasion! COYNAB

CRAY VALLEY PM

Danny Kedwell often talks about being on the lookout for a new 'Gem'. This evening we hear he's giving some youngsters a chance to shine while some established first team regulars rest and prepare for the big FA Cup tie at Chertsey next Saturday. Several youngsters are promise to join the squad for this Kent Senior Cup tie against Cray Valley (PM). Everyone in the car for the drive up to Eltham agrees Cray were the best side in our league last season and thorough deserved promotion. The mood is one of slight trepidation as the Arctic Stadium has not been happy hunting ground for us over recent years. We thought we might have a season off from playing them but no, fate and the Kent Senior Cup draw decided our Tuesday night would mea another trip to south London and the attempt to avoid a repeat of the speeding ticket dished o last time we went there. Will the stadium look any better and will they have any fans this time? We shall see although it's already been noted the entry price has gone up!

They seem to have spent some of their FA Cup and television money from last season on a new food bar, merchandise area and some stands dotted around the place.

hey were superb last season and deserved their success. There is a very sparse crowd to atch this evening and we have a chat with their keeper about why they get so little backing. He lls us that the support is better than it was but there are lots of clubs in the area. We say they serve better support and we can't understand how a club not only survives but seems to be riving on so little support (just 81 here tonight we find out subsequently).

anny Kedwell has decided to play, accompanying two 16 year olds in a back 3. We recognise ax, Adem, Jack, Mikey, Ben Spiers and Johnson Adesanya but all the others are new faces. ay are pretty much full strength given they have relatively light fixture calendar so we're ncerned that this could get ugly!

It turns out we shouldn't have worried, the first half is very even. Yes they are closing us down quickly and giving little time on the ball but our lads are fighting hard; giving as good as they ge No score at half time and people are asking whether or not this goes straight to penalties in the event of a draw so well done us!

We're being forced to defend more and more in the second half and Cray's quality players are showing their pace and quality but we're restricting them to very few clear cut chances. Some our players are looking very tired but nobody can fault the effort being shown. They break through in the 74th minute; a great shot so nearly saved by the diving Ben Spiers. We've used all the substitutes now so that's 9 under 18's on the pitch but generally we hold our own and the two further goals conceded towards the end makes the final 3 nil scoreline suggest a comfortable win. Comfortable it wasn't and it's testament to our young team that the Cray bench celebrate as if they've won the FA Cup.

It's a reasonably happy drive home despite roadworks on the M20 meaning a somewhat circuitous route. We all agree it's pleasing to see some youngsters getting a go especially after the disappointment of the Under 23 side not happening this season. More important is Saturday's FA Cup game at Chertsey obviously but it's a 6 year project to get two promotions so the young lads we watched today have a real chance to be involved with something very exciting. It looks like, from tonight's showing, that the youngsters are up for it! COYNAB!

CHERTSEY TOWN

Our cup run in the FA Cup has nearly got us into October and we're potentially just two games away from drawing a football league team; what's not to get excited about? Another coach trip as well and there's nothing better than a coach load of Nuts and Bolts tourists full of hope and expectation and predictions are ranging from good wins to an away draw. Nobody (except the bookies it turns out) is expecting defeat. Fortunately the rain's stopped, it's a sunny day and the good people at Chertsey have told us that there'll be no need to do a pitch inspection. It's on and all we need to do is negotiate the lottery of the M25.

The ground is in the centre of leafy Chertsey and the coach drops us off nearby in good time and we enjoy some warm sunshine as we admire the beautifully manicured grass pitch. They obviously have a good groundsman and someone who knows how to use a lawn mower!

The team come out into the sunshine to start warming up. They go through some new warmups a mixture of painful looking stretches with big boy elastic bands used as some sort of torture implement and something from the 'ministry of silly walks'! This seems to be the new addition to the squad, Matt Bodkin's doing. He's the fitness coach and latter day Chatham hero that Danny has talked out of retirement to join 'Project AUFC'.

Chertsey give us all a warm welcome and the announcements are very clear and informative. Sustenance is purchased (Burger and cup of tea £7 and a 7 out of 10) and we're all ready now for kick off and the singing starts. A new banner is unveiled celebrating our very own FA Cup Golden Boot hopeful; another hat trick today perhaps?

s only 6 minutes into the game and already we're one down. That looked too easy and they
em to be winning all the second balls and we have no space or time on the ball; it's not going
ll. 2 nil at half time is probably about right and truth be told it could have been worse. Two nil
a dangerous lead we all know but there are lots of concerned faces among the excellent
hford supporters who keep singing anyway.

s the second half and sadly it's not getting any better. The excellent Marley St Louis (still a
eat in the first half) hobbles to the bench clearly injured so an enforced substitution and not
g after kick off we concede a third. It's a mountain to climb now and we're not playing well
wever the faithful behind the goal still believe. Louis is brought down in the box and we get a
nalty. Up steps Gaz and yes he converts his 10th goal of the FA Cup this season. Is there still
me hope?

e of their players has a horrible accident crashing into the wall surrounding the pitch. The
ll looks very close to the pitch from where we're standing but must be legal. There are very
ncerned faces and helpers rush to his aid. The match is suspended for 15 minutes and we all
sh him well and hope he's OK and has a speedy recovery.

e're on top, exposed at the back but on top and pressing hard. There's a goalmouth scramble
d sub Max Walsh scores from 5 yards out; is the comeback on. The singing intensifies behind
e goal and the fans try to suck the ball into the net. The away support today is brilliant. Deep
o the 15 minutes injury time there's another goalmouth scramble; is there a handball there?!
e referee says no and shortly after the referee blows his whistle and our FA Cup run is
ded.

e gave it a good go in the end but clearly we were punished for not getting going for probably
e first 70 minutes of the game. Another 10 minutes and we'd probably have scored but 'what
s' don't count at the end of the day.

ong drive home and there's a mixture of disappointment tinged with the realisation that it was
likely we'd have gone on to win the FA Cup anyway. We'd achieved a decent cup run but it's

a shame we didn't play better today; we simply didn't play the way we know we can. A good day out and we wonder when the next coach trip will happen; soon hopefully COYNAB!

EAST GRINSTEAD

A Tuesday evening after a heavy home defeat on the proceeding Saturday is always a tricky psychological tussle with the old internal dialogue going into overdrive;
'Do I want to go through that again, maybe give it a miss? Don't be daft, they'll need support more than ever. Yes but that feeling on Saturday was horrible so maybe best avoided and it's a long drive? Call yourself a supporter, get a grip man!'

In the end we settle on the 'bounce back Tuesday' hope and there's only one usual tourist not with us (some feeble excuse of a VIP concert at the Albert Hall or something). We leave early as it's a good hour and twenty minutes and East Grinstead insist on kicking off early at 7.30 for some reason. The discussion on the way is akin to a postmortem. Saturday's game is analysed and the conclusion come to that none of us knew where it went wrong, only that it did. Much speculation on squad changes and formations for this one; not only because of Saturday but the forthcoming heavy match schedule. It could be interesting.

As usual we're early and a couple of us don our green and white Christmas hats to counter East Grinstead's association with Ashford United and Christmas (all goes back to when we cancelled the Boxing Day fixture due to Covid in our camp and the feeling is they might have doubted our integrity on the matter?). Anyway, fight fire with fire and hopefully we'll be the ones singing 'oh what fun it is to see Ashford win away' tonight; we certainly need a win! East Grinstead staff are welcoming and friendly as ever and the players start warming up on what must be quite a heavy pitch. It's only waterlogged behind the goals and their ground staff have done a good job. The stand overlooking the ground is high up offering a good view of proceedings for those that want to sit. As it starts to rain it is a shame there's no cover here behind the goal. Fortunately, the rain stops in time for the kick off.

Danny Kedwell replaces Gary Lockyer as Centre Forward; that causes a bit of a stir and there are other changes with Matt Bodkin starting as well. Kick off and we're very much on top and there's only one side going to score here. The Gaffer takes the opening goal very well with his left foot and we're away. We miss chances again; Theo, Will, Dunne and Louis being unselfish but we want them to put their laces through the ball and bury it in the back of the net! Suddenly, they score from nowhere; it's not going to mean we pay the cost of missing our chances again is it? Fortunately Louis scores on the cusp of half time with a beautifully tucked away finish. Thumbs up all round.

The second half is most enjoyable. We're kicking down the hill and dominating. Their Centre Back is sent off for bringing Danny down as the last man and they seemingly have no answer. Then the special moment! All those doubts about whether to come to the game tonight are

brushed aside by a superb, Goal of the Season contender, from the gaffer. You've probably already seen it on social media by the time you read this but if you haven't do yourself a favour and watch it asap. Brilliant goal.
Much singing and smiling faces come the end and we have a chat with an EG supporter in a red and white Christmas hat. He basically confirms what we're all thinking; we were much the better side on the night.
So, the first win in the league this season and it's a start. Eastbourne on Saturday to look forward to and on the drive home we discuss whether or not they'll be comings and goings in the squad, all this punctuated by an unfortunate incident with a back seat tourist and a Tagliatelle which is best not described here. Those who experienced it, will never forget. We all agree that Danny must have loved playing and scoring his two goals and how fit was Matt Bodkin for a 41 year old! Obviously the future is the youngsters and when you look at it we have several teenagers in the squad; how lucky they are to have the opportunity to learn from the experience at the club. Christmas hats away and the internal dialogue re Saturdays drive and game at Eastbourne is already far less fractious. COYNAB

EASTBOURNE

We set off in the wet, however it seems that everyone in the car has been studying weather radar maps and the consensus is that it'll be fine; not only should the game be on but it should be sunny when we get there. It's always a slow and painful drive to Eastbourne no matter what road is taken (How did Rhyle Ovenden do that traveling every week?) However, it's much easier on the back of a great away win last Tuesday. Spirits are high and The East Grinstead win feels significant.
We manage to park in the sports complex where there's a hockey match going on and is obviously Eastbourne's cricket ground in the summer. The ground is suitably cordoned off and has an imposing clock tower backdrop.

The sun's come out and there's a good atmosphere with Eastbourne Town clearly enjoying their promotion to our league. The grass looks long, obviously because of all the rain recently, and the players tell us it's not too bad and quite firm under the wet grass. Refreshments are purchased, hot and cold drinks and burgers, hot dogs etc (7/10 and not overpriced).
During the pre match warm up us tourists are given a firm fitness test! Several times we're forced to break into above average speed walks to retrieve balls (£50 a pop these days

(apparently) from errant shots. The dexterity on show was spellbinding and incredible imagination was displayed to retrieve a ball resting atop a cricket practice net. This is what made Britain Great. The team probably took great motivation from us.

The game's only just started and we're one up! A mishit cross shot from Joey Taylor and the excellent Louis Collins steers the ball into the net; good reflexes there! One day soon we're going to steamroller a team; could it be today?

We are on top and should be more than one up; Louis forcing good saves from their excellent keeper. A short moment of self destruction and they draw level. Hugely frustrating and we couldn't really see what happened exactly and why the ball wasn't easily cleared. At half time we're therefore level. Hopefully, this time we'll come out in the second half and win this one. The sun's out, it's quite warm, there's a horrible drive home ahead; we need to do the business now.

We're pressing hard in the second half and Danny Kedwell turns the screw making impactful changes throughout the 45 minutes. We hit the crossbar, have several corners and their keep keeps making excellent stops. In the end it had to come though didn't it? Matt Bodkin once again is excellent on the right and delivers a pinpoint cross to the forehead of Gary Lockyer; he doesn't miss those and at last we're ahead again. There's a smile on Gary's face and he enjoy that one.

The usual nerve dangling few minutes are endured before the final whistle and that's maximum points from our last two away fixtures; not bad, not too bad at all!

It's a long and slow drive home and choosing a different route didn't really help. Safe to say we're all tired but quite upbeat as it looks like this team is beginning to be just that, a team. There's depth as well and the subs today really helped in the second half. If we can start playi and taking chances at The Homelands then we'll be off and running in the league and next Tuesday night's game against Lancing feels important. Let's hope we keep the momentum ing. Next Saturday's trip to Lewes is a free swing really in the FA Trophy and should be a bit fun but we all want to climb up that league and get into the playoffs; why not? COYNAB.

WES

other long drive to Sussex and whilst we're all disappointed we couldn't get a bus for this e, everyone is really looking forward to visiting Lewes's ground; the famous Dripping Pan. hy is it called the Dripping Pan we ask and the Nuts and Bolts tourist resident historian gives a lesson about the various theories going back in perpetuity. The bottom line is, however, body knows!

ving won three on the bounce in the league and the squad looking better all the time, why ouldn't we give these Isthmian Premier high flyers a game? It's the FA Trophy and a 'free ing' for us and the pressure on them today. It'd be nice to win this.

er a drive that felt easier than last weeks circuitous trek to Eastbourne we arrive in a very sy Lewes town centre. On the way we pass lots of people in their blue and white scarves viously going to the Brighton Wolves game at the Amex. We all agree that we'd far rather tch non league football than shell out a fortune for Premiership tickets, remote from the tion, the players, opposition supporters and the atmosphere that makes following the Nuts d Bolts such an addictive passion. There's nowhere to park (the small paying car park full) ich seems ridiculous given Lewes were a National League side recently. We manage to find mewhere to leave the car at a nearby business; the business seems closed today, there are signs saying we can't park there and no chains across the exit so we're sorted and walk back the ground.

e Dripping pan is a great place to watch football. In a natural dip and with great viewing all und. The hybrid pitch (did someone once say we were getting one of those??) looks ulous. The mix of natural grass and artificial grass means there's a stark contrast between the meadow we played on at Eastbourne last weekend and the short, fast surface that looks perfect for open flowing football; we will see.

There's brilliant behind the goal terracing at both ends of the ground; perfect, not only for a goo atmosphere, but for viewing as well. We're all envious and we all hope that when the AUFC 6 year plan happens and we go up a couple of leagues, we'll end up with a Homelands with terracing at both ends as well. They've also got an all weather big screen which looks brilliant;

For those wanting to sit down to watch the game (Us tourists struggle to get our heads round that concept) there's a bright, modern stand running down one side of the ground as well. Imagine something like this opposite our main stand at the Homelands!

Food and drink is consumed but there are problems as it seems it's mainly card only and some of us only have cash. It's 2024 and most people these days want/expect a choice of card or cash both to get into the ground and to buy food inside. It's a frustration for some but the food looks OK if pricey. Chili Chips for example is £8 (said to be 'not too bad). One tourist, an expert in fast food, isn't happy about the choice saying it's all a bit 'Hipster' for him, all a bit Brighton. He believes that if you go to a football match you should be able to get a burger; a basic human right.

It's that time of the year and obviously the Lewes bonfire celebrations are world famous. One of the numerous Lewes Bonfire societies form a guard of honour for the mighty Nuts and Bolts (oh and the Lewes team are there too);

We've made a few changes for this one with Beckenham, Burgess Hill and Ramsgate fast approaching in the all important League. Marley isn't feeling well apparently and Will Duprey has a well deserved rest and is a sub. Good to see Noah Carny back and on the bench alongside Theo and the very promising Preston Kedwell. Adem, Ronald and Jack all start.

We're on top here and look energetic and creative. We're making a few chances and their keeper has to make some sharp saves. Surely it's only a matter of time before Lewes start imposing their quality on the game but it's the Nuts and Bolts that take a deserved lead. Ronald is finding his feet down the right, linking well with the absolutely superb Matt Bodkin. He fires in a low cross and their unfortunate keeper fumbles and the ball ends up in the net.
Ashford fans keep singing and the Lewes supporters are very quiet as the second half continues in a similar vein to the first.

e get a deserved second goal from a lovely piece of work from Louis; Gary finishing it off.
're two up and still looking the more likely to score. Adem takes a free kick, the ball loops
yond the back post, Gary heads the ball back into the six yard box for a Louis tap in. 3 nil and
ust be all over but wait the linesman puts his flag up and sees an offside. We can't believe
t decision and it feels significant. Tolu goes down injured and has to go off and Lewes wake
 and start peppering balls down our wings. It's the last few minutes and they get one back.
 enter 5 minutes of injury time and Lewes equalise which is heartbreaking.

 the FA Trophy it's straight to penalties (would have been nice for a replay at the Homelands
 nobody needs extra time with Beckenham on Tuesday!). Some excellent penalties are taken
 both sides but in the end Lewes take it 8 7. They celebrate like they've won the FA Cup
ainst a team 35 places behind them in the league pyramid. Ashford fans sing with pride over
reat performance and a Lewes fan stops us as we walk out saying that Ashford deserved to
 today, were by far the better side and if we play like that every week will get promotion. We
h each other the very best for the rest of the season.

The drive home takes longer with traffic in Lewes the Satnav taking us the wrong way and a road closure caused by a fallen tree getting in our way. The mood however is upbeat; if we we going to go out of the Trophy then we all wanted to go out with our heads held high And we certainly did that today. In the end the priority has to be to climb the league table and that's no what we can focus on. The upcoming Tuesday night fixture against table topping Beckenham feels important and after today we can't wait! COYNAB!

BURGESS HILL

The last time we went to Burgess Hill {or Burgers Hill as some of us call it) was just after the club had parted ways with Kevin Watson and Alan Walker had taken temporary charge of the team. Strange times and the only thing remembered from that night was the quality of the Burgess Hill burgers and nobody can remember the match score. Times have changed since then as has the squad with only three players from then with us now. It's a long drive and a couple of usual tourists have made their excuses for this one but it's nothing to do with last Tuesday's Beckenham defeat, however hard that was to take.

Burgess Hill are doing really well this season and are flying high in the league. We're the walking wounded with Tolu, Marley, Joey Taylor, Mikey Berry, Noah all out injured and there's rumour in the car that Ronald Sithole has left already! If we can get something out of today it'l be a bonus.

43

The ground is a fairly typical unspectacular Isthmian league affair but they are always welcoming and seem nice people. Their crowds haven't been too bad recently on the back of their success so the car park's pretty full even though we're early. Hopefully the grounded exhaust pipe of the car in the car park will be ok when we leave!

The lads are warming up in the red away kit. Faces there we don't recognise and the Gaffer is clearly playing today. Terrible news is that on top of all the injuries we find out that the excellent James Dunne can't play today because of suspension (too many yellow cards!). The pitch looks pretty heavy and slopes in different directions. The good news is that the burgers are still excellent here (8.3/10).

Remembrance Sunday soon and the good people of Burgess Hill do an excellent pre match jo[cut] especially the bugler who plays note perfectly. Well done.

Kick off and we're playing ok and holding our own; young Kedwell (Preston) is really worrying them up front with his pace and tenacity. They're strong though clearly and we're having to dig[cut] in and defend. Kedwell Snr (Danny) playing centre half today is making some excellent clearances but they're pushing hard. There's a player bundle and everyone's involved. Presto[cut] and their left back aren't getting on it seems; handbags as they say. The Ref shows a red card[cut] to both which seems very harsh and we go in at half time level with no score.

Second half is about to kick off and Gary's off injured and Jamie Splatt is also replaced. Looks[cut] like Adem and young Jireh George are on. Suddenly we're on the front foot and doing really w[cut] and against all the odds young Jireh George scores! Can we hang on to a lead here? Some o[cut] our players are looking out on their feet and the Gaffer has to finally give in to it and young Alfi[cut] Wincott replaces him. Will Moses forces a superb save from their keeper but truth be told they're pressing hard. Mitch Beeney makes several top saves; could this be our day?

The answer is no, it's not our day. They get a fortunate own goal and score a good second. T[cut] our credit, we continue to fight and try and go forward. Stoney goes forward and goes close b[cut] it's not to be. The small contingent of away supporters have to accept another defeat.

This is a really tough time for the Nuts and Bolts and hopefully our supporters will encourage t[cut] team and help them through it. The drive home is long however the mood isn't quite as downbeat as it was on Tuesday. There are reasons the results aren't going our way and we're[cut] being patient although the next game is against Ramsgate so that'll be a challenge! We really could do with catching a break and we'll see what happens on Tuesday COYNAB!

LANCING

Setting off on the long drive to Lancing we're surprisingly upbeat. The weather is miserable (will we see the sun again?) and we're on a losing streak but there were signs of hope in the last 10 minutes of the loss against odds on favourites Ramsgate on Tuesday. Two late goals and had we had more time left we'd have at least drawn that game. So we're traveling not in expectation necessarily but with hope.

We're early (as always) and are lucky to find a parking place in their car park. Lancing's ground is always neat and tidy, looked after as a base for the Sussex FA. The 3G pitch must be a few years old now but still looks in good nick and is obviously looked after.

We have tea and try the burgers (surprisingly good actually 7.4 out of 10). One tourist seems to be struggling not realising that he's losing a quarter of his burger out the bottom of his roll and ends up surrounded by burger detritus; blissfully unaware. We're attacked by the flock of birds sitting on the floodlight, hats and coats ruined but is it good luck? Didn't feel like it at the time to be honest.

We have 2 new signings Malachi Moses (brother of Maliq Moses who was with us briefly at the end of last season) and the ever young Barry Fuller. It was interesting to see Barry warming up alongside 16 year old Preston (rightly reprieved from his red card suspension against Burgess Hill).

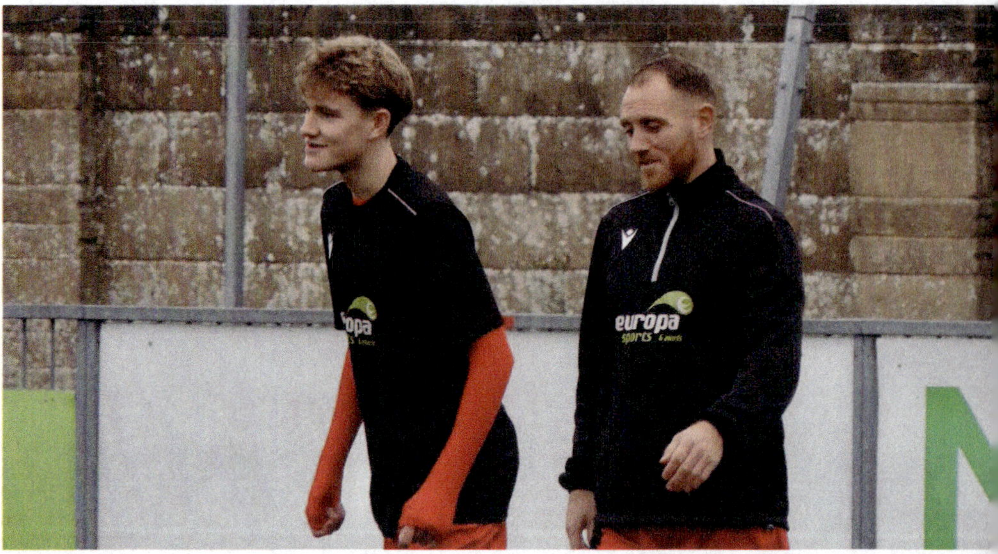
europa
sports

r goalkeeper is obviously too cool to get involved with Matt Bodkin's pre match warm ups it ems.

It's a good game in the first half and pretty end to end. Fun for the neutral but come on Ashfor start asserting your quality please. Jack Saunders does some good work and hits the post; ba luck that. Preston is being a pest as usual and his good work sets up an easy finish for Gary. We're away, now score more and put this to bed. Matt Bodkin is forced off injured and Adem comes on; he's playing left back and at half time we're OK and hopefully we can push on in th second half.

What's happening here in the second half? Why do Lancing look quicker than us all over the pitch, winning second balls and pushing us back? Their equaliser was coming but hopefully it will get us going. We all want Louis to be up front but he's forced back to playing in the midfie it seems. They score a second and the depression around the few Ashford supporters here is palpable. Danny, Malachi and Theo join the fray but it's not happening. Defeat and this one really hurts.

The drive home seems much longer than the drive there and obviously everyone has strong opinions about where the problems lie. Who would want to be Danny right now? The darknes before the dawn hopefully. The mojo is flat, it has to be said; hopefully we'll get it back before Tuesday. The team needs lifting up by the supporters that's clear and hopefully there'll be sor noise against Littlehampton. One thing's for sure we need wins in the 3 upcoming home game to get back on track. COYNAB!

BECKENHAM TOWN

To be completely honest nobody in the car was looking forward to Eden Park where Beckenham play; it certainly puts what we have at The Homelands (now The Green Box Stadium, obviously!) into perspective and we're lucky to have such a home. Storm Bert is hitting Britain as well and we're forecast strong winds and rain, huzzah!

We've had some great league results of late and are gradually climbing the league table however the 'what if' questions in the car are prominent; what if we lose these three tough away games will we be in a relegation fight? But what if we win them, does that mean we'll be pushing the play off places by Christmas? One game at a time.

We're all a bit under the weather (colds, chest infections, getting old etc) and one of our crew doesn't pass his fitness test to make the journey. We're not that unwell so it's a surprise when the main topic of conversation on the 90 minute drive seems to be about near death experiences and the disappointment that none of us tourists had experienced one! Perhaps, with hindsight, it's a good thing that we haven't.

The houses as we approach the ground are obviously of high value so there's a huge contrast when we enter the ground.

The pitch looks good anyway. We get a cup of tea and are given fun size Mars Bars (at full price!) and we don't risk the food. It's blowing a gale out there from left to right and this could be horrible to watch; hopes are not high!

Spirits drop further as we go one down; it's only five minutes into the game and it looks a soft goal as well. This is not making us feel any better! We're digging in and working out how to play to the wind and putting up a fight. Beckenham have two or three wonderfully skilful players on the ball and their player known as 'magic' is showing off with flicks and no look passes. Hard to admit but they're actually quite good to watch and it's turning into an enjoyable game. But we have some good players as well and Mikey forces a great save from their keeper. We're doing OK and Jack puts in a great cross and Gary scores a trademark diving header equaliser! Smile on faces; perhaps it was a good decision to get out of our sick beds after all!

At halftime, honours are even and this is a much better game than anyone expected. We have the wind in our sails in the second half, metaphorically and literally and we're on top. Dunne is brilliant as usual albeit close to a second yellow card at times but this is his type of game clear Youngsters Mikey and Jack are both doing great but it's Barry Fuller (at the other end of his footballing career) that supplies the cross for Gary's second headed goal; get in! Gary is broug down and Dunne doesn't miss from the penalty spot. The nervous tension isn't there today (it usually is when we're ahead afraid of a fight back) as we keep attacking, keep fighting and we go close another couple of times. The wind is howling and the rain pouring but nobody seems notice or care when the final whistle goes. Well done, that's what we want to see and we're gla we came! It's a good drive home and we're looking forward to another trip to Deal on Tuesday night and wouldn't it be great if we can keep this league run going COYNAB!

DEAL TOWN

So we recently inherited an 8 year old cat following a bereavement. It's been let out for the firs few times recently and for reasons best known to the swine animal it decided to stay out as leaving time approached. With nobody else at home this evening what was to be done? Do we not go to the Charles Sports Ground in Deal to encourage the mighty Nuts on Bolts to hopeful a fourth win on the trot or is the right thing to do try and find the moggy? Decisions decisions.

On the way to Deal our recent form and the great win at Beckenham on Saturday has filled the car with optimism. We've left a little late so are relieved to find one remaining space to park. Deal have enjoyed good support for a little while now and are enjoying their promotion to our league. We like the Charles Ground (a contrast to Eden Park!), it's nice enough, has a good (overly bright) scoreboard and the people are friendly and welcoming.

Craig Stone scored the only goal when we were here a couple of months ago in the FA Trophy or did he? Some say it was an own goal but we gave it to the skipper.

Will Dupray isn't here tonight and Mack Riley (we like Mack), Harrison Hume, Dean Beckwith, Matt Bodkin and young Alfie Wincott have been drafted in to reinforce the bench. We hear that James Dunne is playing tonight before starting a two match suspension (10 yellow cards) which is really bad news for the Merstham game on Saturday! One game at a time though and the selection looks bold with young Preston coming in for Will Dupray. Let's keep this going.

Tea's and assortments consumed (several outlets all around the ground here at reasonable prices) we get going. We've started off playing with a high degree of confidence. The shape looks good and you can tell it's a settled side now. This is really good stuff and we get our reward and the 'pest' Preston gets his first goal for the Nuts and bolts!

Three minutes later and Gary scores another cracker with his head (doesn't need football boots these days, just scoring exclusively with his head!). Deal are rattled and are arguing amongst themselves and we always like to see that. They're a good side however and the FA Trophy game earlier in the season was a close game. They fight and get some dangerous crosses in but Mitch Beeney isn't really troubled. We've made it to half time and there are smiles on faces behind the Ashford goal.

![Scoreboard showing Deal Town 0, Ashford United 2, time 47]

a hard fight in the second half and Mikey Berry even gets booked. Suddenly there's a big
nalty appeal but it's outside the box surely. No, it's given and Macca Murray (son of Paul
rray ex AUFC coach) puts it away. Oh no, they're not going to do the classic comeback from
) down are they? Tension and concern but we're fighting hard.

e second half seems much longer than it should and in the 83rd minute Craig Stone volleys
me! He must really like this place as it's the same goal he scored into earlier in the season.
lief and joy behind the goal; we're on a streak of four league wins on the bounce and a well
served win as well. We're looking good just now.

The rain starts as we leave fortunately and we're delighted. Merstham could well prove to be toughest of the three games this week on Saturday but we're on a roll now so why not keep th going COYNAB

ps The cat was waiting for our return and is absolutely fine!

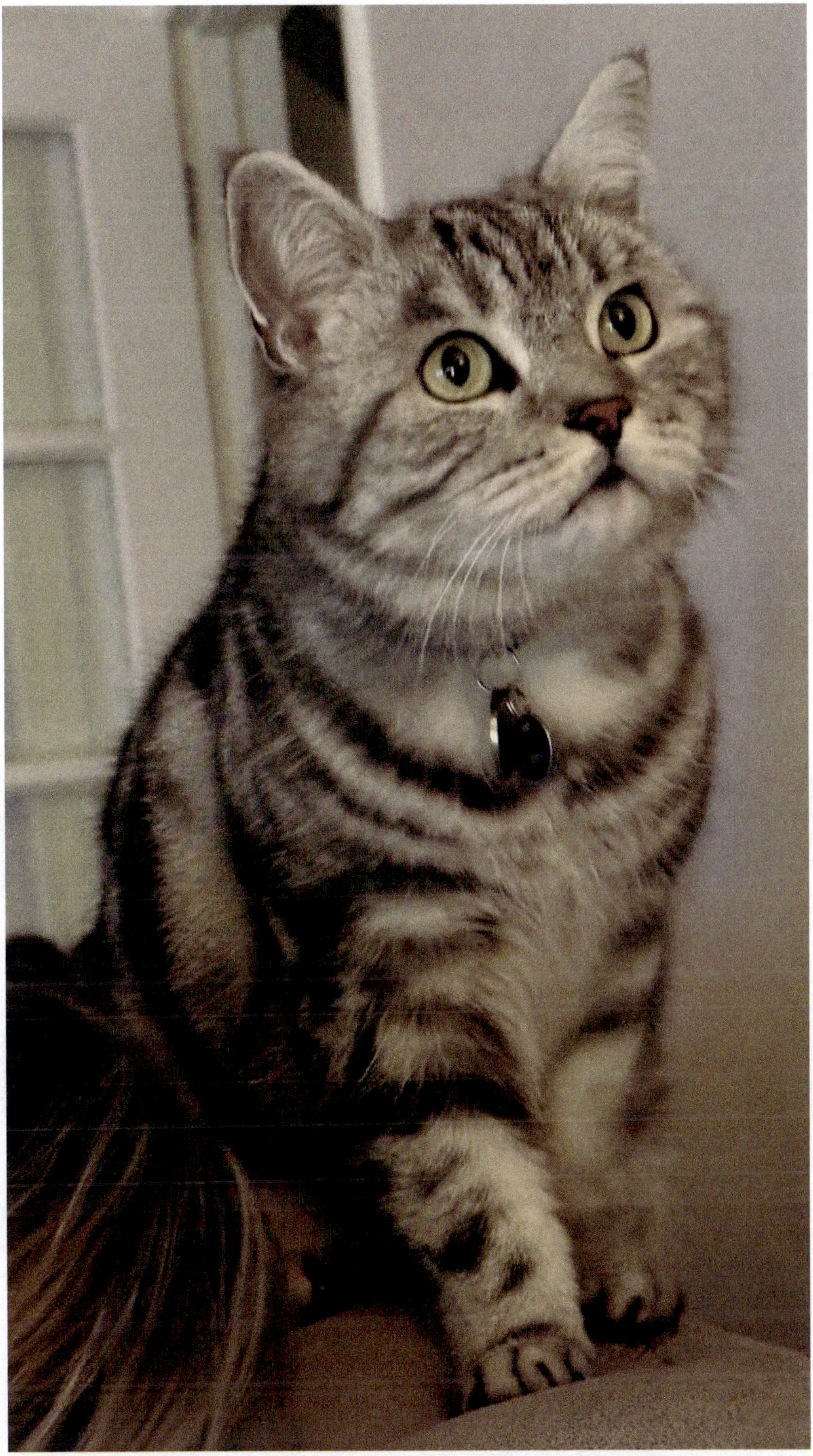

MERSTHAM

The rollercoaster of emotions following AUFC continues. Four good wins in the league and it all feels on the up however we wake up to another 'sky on your head' day and the M25 in prospect for the trip to Merstham. The drive takes too long really; how long are they going to keep taking the M26 to one lane as it joins the M25? The drizzle has started and James Dunne is suspended for this one. The atmosphere in the car could be a little more positive truth be told and we'd all be happy with a draw today.

Having only been here once before (they were promoted to our league last season) we'd forgotten there's nowhere to park so we join the numerous vehicles upsetting the locals by parking on the pavement and trudge our way towards the floodlights; mud everywhere and all very non-league. Warm welcome at the gate and we're told where to get refreshments and programmes and we're in and the lads are already warming up. Our mug of tea is OK this season as last season the surface slick made it memorably unappetising; this season all good and the Mars bars don't come from a party bag!

We have a new player on loan from Dartford, Gabe Campbell and he has a reputation for being rapid. Joey Taylor is back on the bench and whilst Noah Carney is here it's just too soon still for a run out today. For a small village, Merstham seem to get good support and there's a decent crowd here. The pitch looks heavy and we need the lights on asap as it's so gloomy today.

We've started well and William Dupray is playing in the James Dunne role and we have Preston and Gary up front with Louis playing just behind them. We're the better side here clearly so let's get some chances on goal. Twenty minutes have flown by but Dupray goes into a tackle and looks like he's taken off. It looks bad and sure enough the ref gives him a straight red. Some are saying 'no complaints' others that he was out of control but some are saying he didn't touch him. Being so far away from the incident I guess we'll never know but that's leaving a hole in our midfield now and it could be a long afternoon.

Our boys certainly have character and fight hard; are we sure we're the team with ten men? The referee is having a nightmare and the Merstham players are not endearing themselves to the Ashford support going down in agony if anyone breathes on them. Their Captain Matt Drage is leading by example and goes down with what must be a broken leg half a dozen times and it's disgraceful really. Looks like Danny has had a disagreement with the referee and isn't allowed back to the dugout for the second half.

They're one up and against 10 men but still wasting time and going down as if shot every five minutes. We've risen above it and are still the better side and pushing hard without creating many clear chances. Campbell comes on and looks lively; his first touch almost creating a chance. Joey Taylor comes on and his left foot goes to work testing the Merstham defence but they keep us out. We all believe we'll get a point here as we continue to push but in the 89th minute what happened there? Against the run of play we concede what looks like a very soft goal and the Merstham crowd are celebrating as if they'd won the FA Cup. That's that then.

What a miserable day all in all but at least the motorway jams seem to have cleared. We're all glad that our team doesn't play like Merstham and seem to have better standards. Merstham's number 5 in particular is obviously a man who's realised that dignity is overrated. We'll draw a line under our opponents performance and look forward to annihilating them at the Green Box as Karma will surely out when they come back to ours.
Consensus in the car is that we will be desperate to bounce back hard on Tuesday evening against AFC Croydon and we're looking forward to that one. COYNAB

SHEPPEY UNITED

After a long week waiting for the next match (what no Tuesday game!) we set off with more hope than expectation to play on the Island against Sheppey United, a place where we've not had the best of fortune over the years. Two of today's tourists had a very late night at Trading Boundaries last night (watching the superb Steve Hogarth perform) and are feeling worse for wear, however after two weeks of gloomy and depressing weather we suddenly find ourselves looking up at blue sky and there's a yellow ball in the sky; that feels better! Consensus is that we'd take a draw today and anything else would be a bonus. Looks like Holm Park has had a name change again:-

get something to drink but no Mars bars! Food available but said to be 'a bit pricey'. Lots of
ndly people there and a very good smattering of Nuts and Bolts supporters. Holm Park is
ll kept, a lovely pitch that you look down on and they must be financially in a good place
owing their televised cup run last season. They always seem to do well against us, especially
home, so today looks like being a real test in the setting sun. Not much of a breeze and chilly
it's all set for a good match hopefully.

 say hello to Gil Carvalio who's having a good season with 'The Ites' and he didn't play for us
g enough. We also say hi to an ex Ashford favourite 'The Portuguese Roundabout' Mamadou
llo who is firmly established now as one of Sheppey best players (how did we let him go?).
 too have a very good squad and with recent additions we have depth as well. We learn of
other new signing, Ronnie Vint. The fact that he's well known off the telly (something called
ve Island) leaves us cold and hopefully his 100% focus will be on his defensive duties at
lm Park Sheerness as opposed to 'pitching woo' on Mallorca! We shall see. No Stoney today
d still no Joey Taylor who may be out for a few weeks.

This is a very good game of football; end to end stuff. Sheppey don't seem to be able to handl the ever young Matt Bodkin down the left and the actually young Gabe Campbell down the rig Both have good efforts that just miss and Gabe wins a penalty. Maybe a bit of a soft one but who cares! James Dunne steps up and their keeper makes a great save to his right but fortunately our Dunne is sharp enough to put the rebound away. They're getting back into the game and missing some good chances. They're very quick on the break and score following a rare Bodkin mistake. This could go either way and must be exciting to watch as a neutral. Jus on the stroke of halftime Gary Lockyer (who'd been very quiet up until now) latches on to a ha chance and effectively lobs their keeper and we go in 2-1 up. Gabe is having an excellent gam for us and is a constant threat down the right and teams up well with Jack Saunders who com on at half time for the injured Barry Fuller. Several chances at both ends and a couple we should have put away. Louis Collins is a couple of inches wide but somehow today feels like c day. The lads are cheered home (Will Dupray joins the Ashford massive behind the goal; probably so he gets to hear his song) and we do more than hold out for a well deserved win.

...ppy faces all around and we're all looking forward now to the Christmas fixtures starting on ... 21st against Phoenix (who we really need to beat given results last season!). Things do ... m to be on the up and on the drive home we discuss how many points we realistic need over ... next few games. We believe we can win the majority of the coming games but as Danny ... s 'one game at a time!' COYNAB!!

THE TOWN

The Victorians are responsible for many of the traditions around Christmas, including Boxing Day. The name derives from the tradition where servants were given the day off and received special Christmas Box from their Lords and masters. Some say (well Nick anyway) the name derives from Alms boxes collected by the Church and handed to the poor of the Parish the day after Christmas, who knows. Our Pagan forefathers celebrated by recognising the winter solstice with the promise of shorter nights and longer days to come. Now, of course, this time of the year is all about who the Nuts and Bolts will be playing come Boxing Day. This year we celebrate a local (ish) derby against Hythe Town. Much anticipated and all roads lead to Reachfields for the 1 O'clock kick off.

Mistakenly some of us thought Hythe now had a 3G pitch given it's been like playing on a ploughed field previously. It turns out that last summer the pitch was obviously re-laid and it's still grass. It still looks like there's an elephant that's been buried in the six yard box which means Mitch Beeney will be looking down on the game even more than usual! Today's pitch looks heavy; just what we need given we're playing two games in three days. Some of us thought Reachfields would look a bit different given the change of ownership and promised investment however it looks pretty much the same as always and Hythe are having a shocker a season so far with a terrible -33 goal difference and languishing in the relegation zone. Hopefully we should win this one but we thought the same against Phoenix!

The first half unfortunately is like the weather today, a bit dull with little happening. Unfortunately we lose Will Moses with a hamstring injury which is a shame as he's pretty much been ever present this season and a rock at the back. Half time is upon us with little to report; maybe too much Christmas Pud, who knows.

We've come out of the blocks much the better for whatever was said in the dressing room and the intensity levels are much improved. We're playing well now. The ball comes into the box and Gary Lockyer produces an excellent volley that nearly bursts the net and we're away. We're much the better side and Hythe, it has to be said, are really poor. Not sure where Hythe are going wrong as they have some very good players (their skipper Lex Allen, Medy Elito, Vance Bola and David Ozobia for example) but frankly who cares especially when the ever reliable Olu makes it two. We're not going to let this two goal lead slip, that's for sure.

290 odd people (many of them Ashford fans) are left in no doubt who the better side are today and our Christmas gift is a much needed win (after Phoenix) and a clean sheet. On the way home we're pleased. Obviously we'll be without Gary (suspended) and Will Moses for Erith, Sittingbourne and Steyning Town but if we can average 2 points a game for the rest of the season we'll be there or there about. We also agree we quite like a 1 O'clock kick off.

By the time you read this we'll be through the Christmas and New Year period and will have a much better view of our prospects for the rest of the season but we're doing OK as of now especially with so many players out injured or suspended. We had a Merry Boxing Day anyway COYNAB.

STEYNING TOWN

After wins against Hythe and Erith over the Christmas period and what felt like a win against league leaders Sittingbourne (1-1) hopes are high and everyone is up for the long drive down to somewhere in West Sussex and Steyning Town; a club currently propping up the league. A good win today and we'll be reasonably placed for a late season charge to the playoffs. We need to be ruthless, improve our goal difference and build our confidence levels even more.

It's another miserable day but at least it's not raining. Can this actually be it, we ask as we arrive at a village miles from anywhere? It is, apparently and there's very little parking available. This must be it though as there's some murals painted on some old garages outside that give the game away;

Not much hope of a decent crowd here today and it seems mostly Nuts and Bolts supporters turning up in the cold. Basic facilities are on offer but at least the small 3G pitch looks in good condition and they have LED floodlights as well.

...is place reminds us how lucky we are to have such excellent facilities back at the Green Box ...adium.

...am news is out and it's a surprise that Mikey Berry is on the bench but probably because of ... incredible efforts he's been making on the pitch recently and at the end of the day we don't ...nt him injured. The team looks strong enough and whilst there's talk of injuries and ...spensions the team on the pitch today should be more than good enough to win today.

...ey start defending well and we don't seem to be able to penetrate despite our possession. ...uis Suddenly gets through and rounds the keeper but agonisingly his finish hits the post. The ... rebounds out to Preston who misses his kick and before we know it the guilt edged chance ...ake the lead is gone. What's this now, they've just scored from a set piece and we're one ...wn. This wasn't in the script at all. We hand them a second with a terrible error and we're two ...vn going into the break. Worse thing is, we deserve to be losing.

...ere's an immediate reaction after halftime. Mikey is on and before we know where we are we ...nage two quick goals finished by Preston. That's better, we're on our way now and all is ...given for the first 45 minutes. There's only one team winning here and it's just a case of how ...ny now, surely. Danny is clearly brought down by their keeper; not given for some reason ...d then another effort by Preston looks to be over the line especially given the goal has moved ... inches behind the goal line. But again no. Come on Ashford, a draw's not good enough ...ay, let's get that third. Then disaster and oh no, another mistake; they're through and score. ...at a horrible feeling this is and when the final whistle goes the gloom behind the goal is ...gible.

... a very long drive home and defeat today feels significant for our season. Saturday against ...ee Bridges feels a long way away as well and also is now a must win game. One tourist ...s into full excuses mode; the referee, our injuries and suspensions etc and whilst there's ...ne validity in these comments the other passengers in the car seem less keen to jump on ...t bandwagon today. Reality is that when we start going up through the leagues (it's a when and not an if) we will win these sort of games ruthlessly. We see that Ramsgate beat Three Bridges today 0-5 and we wonder how many of their first team squad were unavailable today and how many referee decisions went against them? Maybe we need the darkness to better se the light but wow this one hurts today.

The talk quickly turns to what's for dinner tonight but we also wonder what Danny will do to make the necessary changes he eluded to post match. The gossip is about the new as yet unnamed midfielder but also whether we will see anyone leave this week. We will see next Saturday however in the meantime we all agree we need to be winning most of our games fro here on in if we seriously want something to play for this season. Saturday's game is now hug COYNAB.

SEVENOAKS

The Nuts and Bolts On Tour soap opera continues with a trip to Sevenoaks, a venue we know well. It's usually a good game at The Bourne Stadium on their nice pitch however unfortunatel we're not expecting a large crowd and we can't understand why Sevenoaks FC don't get more support. One tourist suggests it's because they're a Rugby town but with their population the club, like ours, deserves far more support than it gets. The tourists today have just about got over last week's debacle although one of our number has decided to give today's trip a miss. our experience the total depression that sets in after a bad result and performance usually sta to ease by Tuesday however there's still a hangover in the car today. We're cheered up by ne signings this week (always gives us hope) and there's speculation that another will be reveale today if they've managed to do the paperwork.

We arrive and park at the Bourne Stadium stupidly early and head in in search of a warm cup on another miserably cold day. A small gaggle of AUFC supporters gather for a pre match cha (what is the collective noun for a gathering of Nuts and Bolts supporters? A hope, a spanner, answers on a postcard please).

mbers are down today behind the goal but the match is pretty end to end to start with and at st we can make out the two teams after last week's kit clash. We have new players today, the per, the left back and a new winger who played for West Ham under 18's!

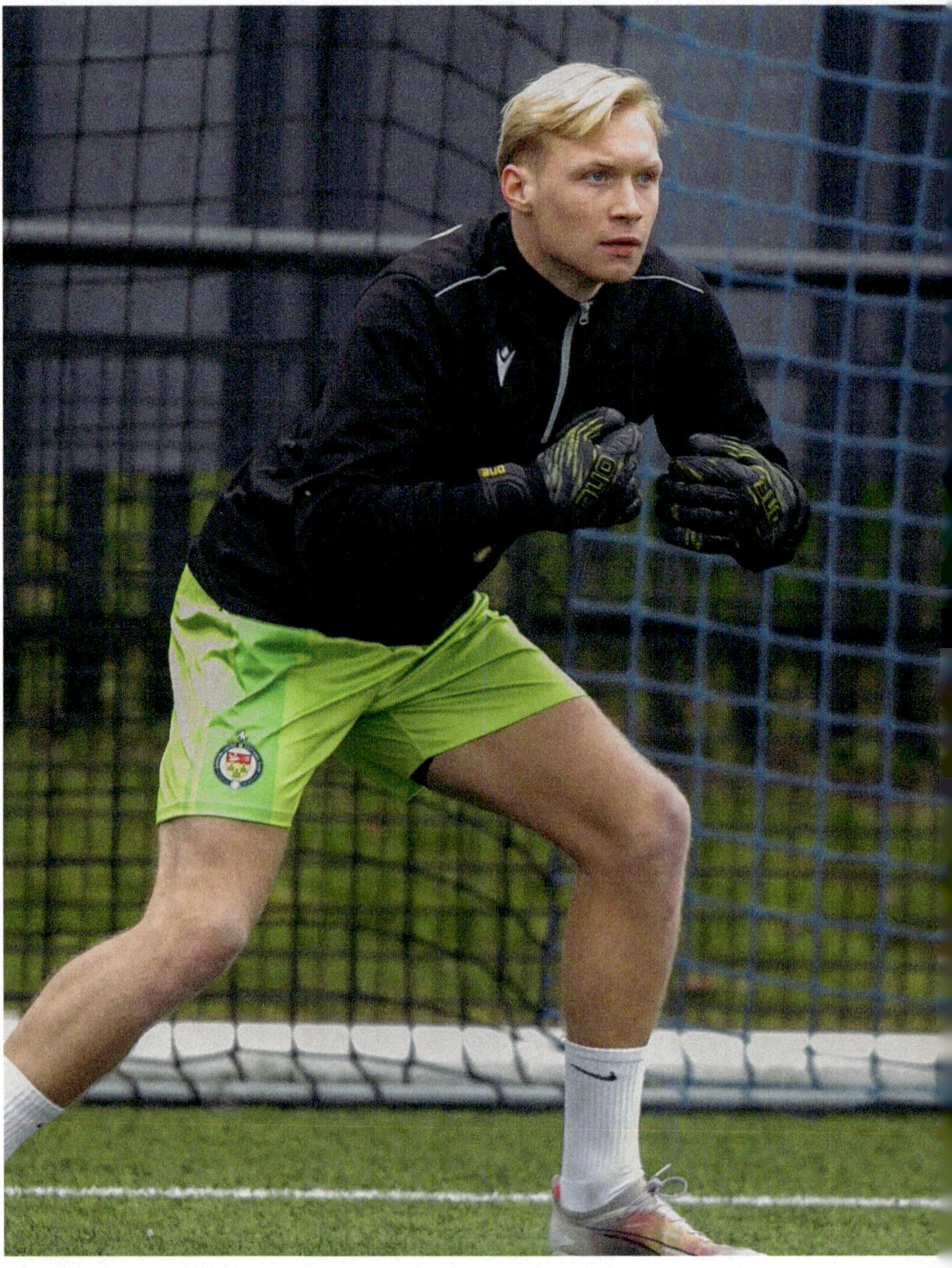

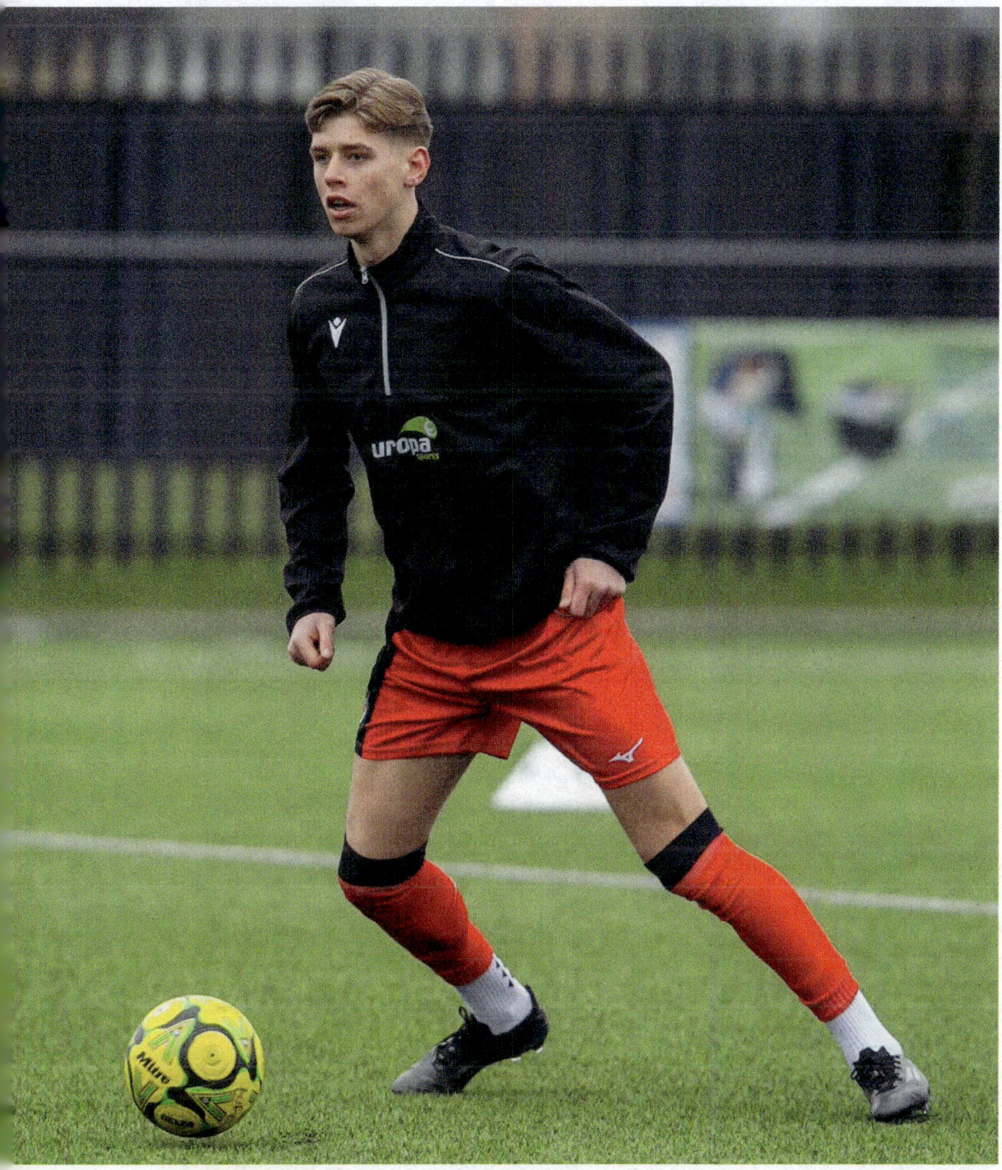
uropa
sports

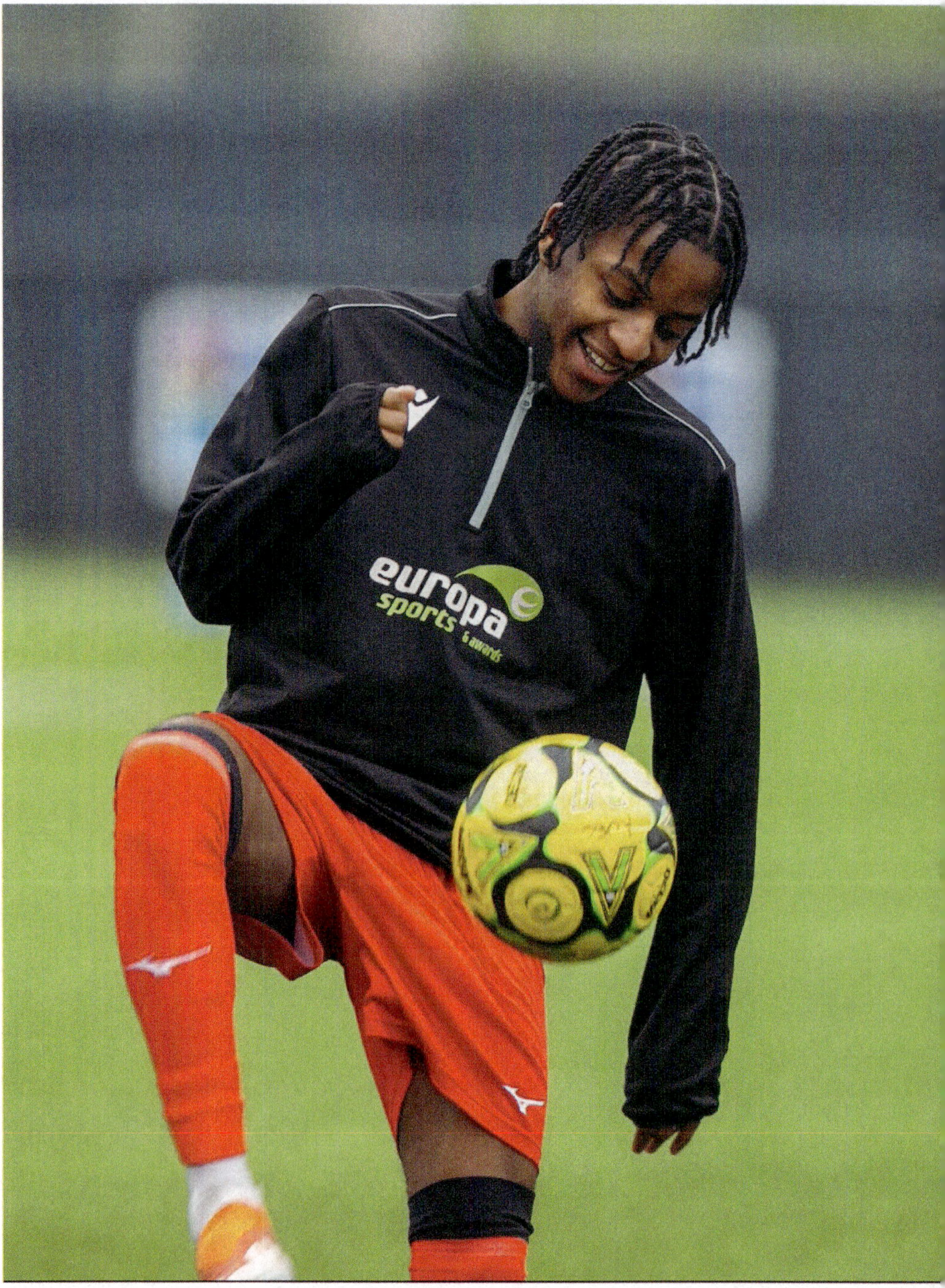
europa
sports
& awards

e've switched ends at the toss so kicking up the slight slope in the first half. End to end and 're giving as good as we get but Sevenoaks seem to be a team well drilled and full of nfidence. We nearly manage to score but the angle into their goal is too acute and they anage to clear off the line. Soon after our chance Sevenoaks score from a cross despite the st efforts of our new keeper. Towards the end of the half they score a second so 2-0 at lftime; we're not getting any luck these days.

we change ends the weather gets colder and everything seems dark and gloomy but we still ve hope that kicking down the slope we'll get back into this.

hope only lasts two minutes when they score an excellent third. To our credit nobody gives and the work ethic is beyond question. Young Blaise Uwandji (ex West Ham) is introduced Michael West with what looks like a hamstring injury unfortunately) and he looks good. We re a deserved goal from some excellent improvisation from Gary Lockyer and a backheal. 're never going to get back into this however and ex Ashford player Ryan Sawyer looks nense at the back for the Oaks. It's also good to see ex AUFC hero Josh Wisson enjoying his tball still in the midfield, still playing with a smile on his face.

els like a long drive home and things aren't going well For our team obviously at the ment. We have good players and it will get better, everyone knows that, but it looks like this son's challenge for promotion is all but over even for the most positive Tourist. Merstham t Saturday and we'll put things right then; COYNAB.

RNE BAY

Last Sunday, after the Merstham defeat, one die hard and long standing fanatical Nuts and Bolts tourist announced he'd basically had enough. There was talk of a season ticket next season at Orient, Millwall or even Charlton (not Ashford!) with the time and expense of following AUFC to away matches being saved; better to be invested in better, quality family time. There was nothing that could be said to placate the chap and this sad state of affairs only amplified the post loss depression prevalent among many of us in green and white. 'Blue Monday' is a real thing apparently (must be true because Naga Munchetty said so on the BBC) so this is the epicentre of a long and difficult winter. We're desperate to see the green shoots of recovery and will they emerge against the old enemy Herne Bay at what they now call 'The Crest Stadium' and will there be 3 or 4 of us in the car this time given our 'had enough' tourist?

All four of us turn up in Herne Bay (yes he came) ridiculously early (as usual) and are raring to go on a beautiful, sunny winter's day. The early kick off (1.30 because they can't use their floodlights at the moment) means it shouldn't get too cold. The pitch looks great, no excuses today. Our wavering tourist was encouraged by the signing of Jack Dixon and reports received of positive training sessions and positivity in the camp so he was with us as usual (thoughts of another clubs season tickets pushed to the back of his mind for now and certainly not discussed today!)

It looks like we managed to sign Kane Diedrick-Roberts as well as he's on the bench today it seems but we're still short with no Michael West, Louis Collins, Will Moses, Will Dupray and Joey Taylor. We all look forward to seeing how Jack 'Dicko' Dixon gets on and all agree what good signing he is.

e announcer calls us Ashford Town grrrrrr and Football Web Pages is saying James Dunne is
ying for us today (a mistake subsequently amended dashing our forlorn hopes that maybe
re had been a last minute rapprochement between Club and player). It's a good crowd
ugh enjoying the weather and the occasion.

're edging the game in the first half and it's a shame to see Harrison Hume injured and
laced which has upset our shape it seems. Noah is having a good game (celebrating his
:h game for Ashford) and we're bright and breezy. Herne Bay then go and score from a
ner against the run of play but it's OK we look like we can at least get back into this. One
vn at the break but the admittedly diminished in numbers Ashford support is not too
vnhearted.

ets harder when Herne Bay go and score another but we still have hope. This score line
is unlucky. Gary, with an excellent finish, pulls one back and we manage to hit the post twice
I we're not getting any luck here. It's all Ashford but then they manage to score a third and
t's that; we can't seem to catch a break at the moment. It's the hope that kills you sometimes.

e drive home is made more difficult by the car in front driving at a solid 29 mph all the way
n Favershambles to Ashford and the journey is a long, drawn out affair. Two desperate
rists endeavour to lighten the mood and distract themselves with, it has to be said, somewhat
orative and misogynist attempts at humour which is disappointing. They must be ashamed
after another defeat today the feeling is their sins can probably be understood (if not
jiven) and they know who they are.

ere's talk of at least two players returning next Saturday and maybe another couple of
nings in the week. The Deal match now feels really important, we need a win and we
sperately need to see those green shoots of recovery soon. It'll be alright in the end and if it's
alright, it's not the end, COYNAB.

OADBRIDGE HEATH

One of our number says he's in two minds about the trip today. It's cold, damp and where exactly was Broadbridge Heath again? We're all here, however, and we're going and although forementioned tourist is not 'up for it' particularly, the win last week has given new hope and at the end of the day we're Nuts and Bolts supporters and it has to be done.

Stanley Skipper is back with us again (with all that Lampard DNA) so that's good news but it's shame that we've heard Westie isn't 100% and Tommy Penfold's been ill. Predictions range from 5-1 to either side (not sure how that works and it's wondered whether everyone is taking things seriously) to 2-1 to us. No real rain recently has meant that we reckon the game's on as we start the journey to West Sussex.

There's tarmac to park on and we're here (very early as usual). The clubhouse is neat and tidy but that's pretty much all they have here and the pitch is looking heavy; hope the team is fit today.

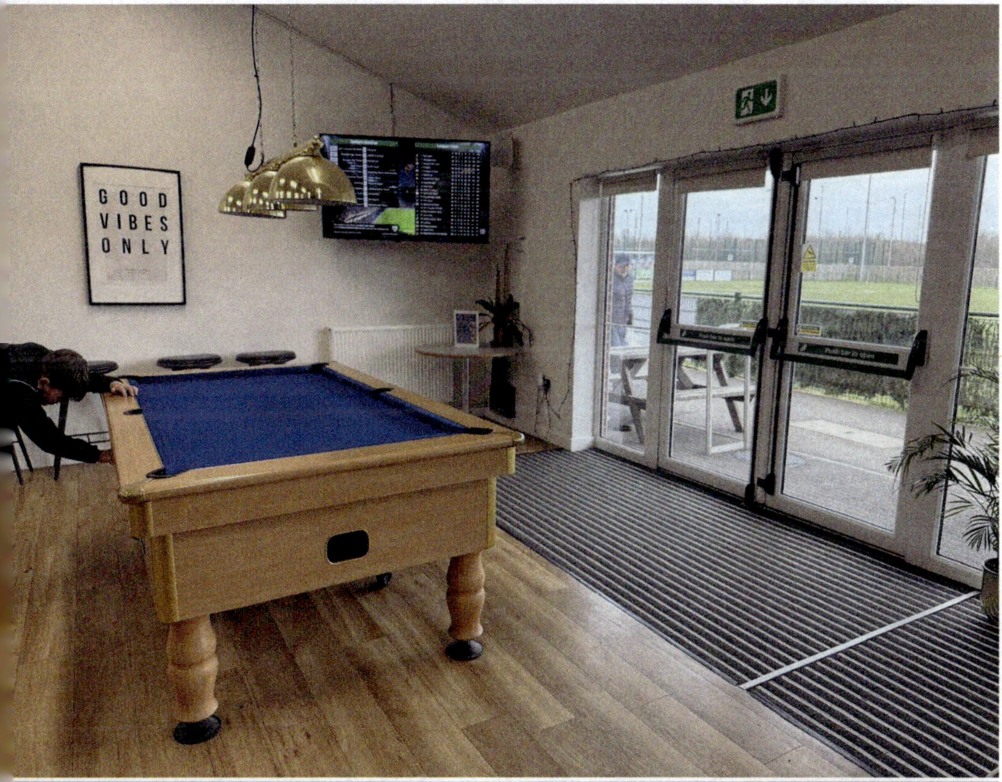
GOOD
VIBES
ONLY

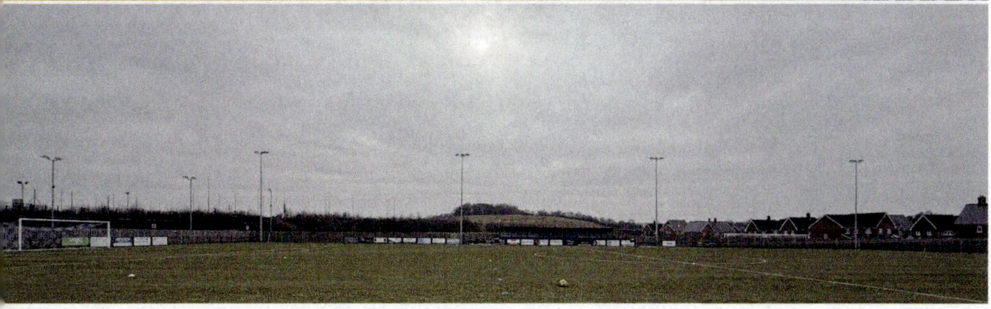

We start like a train and there's a headed flick from Gary and Louis gives us an early lead. Nice start, let's keep this going. It's all getting a bit scrappy and both sides are trying really hard, battling against the conditions and probably cancelling each other out. Pretty it's not and then, out of the blue the 'Bears' are awarded a penalty and it's all square again. We're denied a handball penalty for some reason and at halftime we're equal. Some are saying we need width some are saying we're too light and outnumbered in the midfield and others are OK with it give the conditions and expected a fight like this. All agree the ref seems to be making odd decision and handing yellow cards out for fun and will there be 22 players on the pitch at the end of this

Second half and they score from a corner (Lloyd won't be happy about that!). As the half progresses Broadbridge miss several good chances and to be fair should be more ahead and have just missed a penalty as well! Our fitness is beginning to show, however, and our fight as well; we're not about to give this one up. Gary heads against the post but is quick to react on th floor and scoops home the equaliser. We're going for an unlikely win and Tolu's curling shot is just deflected behind by a Heath defender; that was going in. Gary's miss hit shot is deflected Tolu onto the post; so close.

When the final whistle goes we take a draw and a hard won point away from home. Not a beautiful game today. Both sets of players must be knackered after that fight and again it make us grateful for the playing conditions and support we enjoy at home.

The drive home is wet and long and unfortunate behaviour by one backseat tourist makes the journey more uncomfortable for everyone else; heavy sigh. One among us starts talking about how many points we're off a play off place and is quickly slapped down by everyone else. One game at a time and let's play well, to a system with a solid core of a team and see where it es us. We're looking forward to the free friendly on Tuesday evening and there's speculation to what the team will look like and we'll all be there for the Eastbourne game. Just 11 league mes to go now so not long to go now. COYNAB

C CROYDON

rmzy and Wilfred Zaha; the owners of AFC Croydon apparently. One's a modern poet, we're d and the other owner plays in Turkey now but both must be pretty loaded and maybe their estment helped Croydon to promotion last season. Surely they've been investing in the club astructure and facilities as well? We're looking forward to going to a new ground, anyway d it promises to be a tough match. It takes about 45 minutes to do 3 miles and that's normal und Thornton Heath and Croydon and Florence (the cars Sat Nav) takes us down tight ds, through terraced housing estates to an unwelcoming dirt track with a sign that suggests 're in the right place. The pot-holed track we're forced to go down is adorned with fly tippers ritus and is only passable with extreme care! Is this it? It can't be, can it? It is and we can see floodlights and a stand. Good grief, it doesn't look like the owners have spent anything on ground at all and the tiny car park is quickly filled. It's a good job we're always early and nage to park, just. We're very thankful that the Green Box is like Wembley compared to this ce.

The news doesn't get any better when we look at the playing surface and it's pretty obvious w so many games have been postponed this season. Again, people moan about our artificial surface but we know where we'd like to have played back in the day and where we like to wat decent football now and it's not on this. The good news is that it's a beautiful sunny day.

The attempt to buy a cup of tea and a burger becomes a long drawn out affair. Some of our party were clean shaven when they joined the queue and by the time the cash was exchange for a 3/10 burger (£5) stubble was showing. It's not going too well.

Danny Kedwell, Dean Beckwith and James Dunne all say hi during the warm up and what's gone is gone and everyone is getting on with it now. Unfortunately we have several missing through suspension and injury but the good news is Michael West is back but on the bench to start with.

're giving as good as we get as eventually we get started and it's pretty even, hard fought
few chances. The difference here seems to be, the ball is falling for them and not us and
y have a couple of chances that they take well. Two down at half time feels a little cruel as
re every bit as good as them but the scoreboard doesn't lie.

The second half is all Ashford. Joey Taylor (fresh from a dislocated shoulder on Tuesday night) is substituted as the half goes on as is Matt Bodkin. Tommy Penfold is playing centre forward and working hard. Harry Waldock picks up the ball in his own half and runs forward well putting the ever willing Louis Collins in down the left. The maestro cuts back onto his right foot and slots a much deserved goal into the corner. This is good Ashford, this is better and we deserve something out of the match. The ball comes high into the box and Tommy heads on beautifully into the path of Michael West who hits the ball just too well and it goes over the bar agonisingly. That feels significant but what a good player he is just to have got into that position. It's just not our day today but it easily could have been. 2-1 in the end; so near unmet so far.

Some were expecting much more from Croydon but they were fortunate to edge it in the end. We're looking forward to firstly getting out of this 'stadium', negotiating the mud track and fighting our way out of Thornton Heath. Florence pulls off a master stroke and as a result the journey home feels not too bad. The tourists don't feel too bad either. Yes the boring negative comments will probably flow online but who cares; we'll be positive, we'll support the lads and we'll say it as we see it; 'promising'. The small matter of Burgess Hill next; a team that hasn't lost for ages but we'll have a big, available squad for that one so we're looking forward to the challenge. COYNAB.

PHOENIX SPORTS

Two wins in a row and a squad looking stronger by the week; what's not to like as we hit the M20 for the day we put things right with Phoenix! We've played them on 22 occasions but only won four times. It's a ridiculous stat given that they're a yo-yo team with regular relegations and promotions. This year they're fighting to stay up again and it looks like it'll either be them or Littlehampton that go down. In the car we all hope it's Littlehampton that go down (we don't like Littlehampton) but that doesn't mean we want to lose today. It's getting embarrassing and if we're serious about being top three next season, we need to be winning against teams like Steyning, Lancing and Phoenix.

How do clubs like Phoenix survive financially? Seriously, they get no support and the facilities are basic to say the least. We always try to provide a couple of photos of away grounds (for people that don't travel) however these are all we could come up with this week:-

The pitch looks very rough and bumpy. However it's dry and we're reassured to learn that the dog mess on the right wing has been successfully cleared up prior to kick off. Burgers score a good 8 out of 10 as does the beer (£4.80 a pint apparently). The sausage rolls (£2) however quickly become a case of 'buyer's remorse' and even though this blog is being written 24 hours later it's still being remembered on a regular basis! The ladies in the tea shop are very friendly though and they're making the best of it. Hopefully nobody is going to pick up a serious injury from playing on that pitch today (or eating the sausage rolls).

We're in red today and it's a strong looking side. Tolu, Noah, Will Dupray, Matt Bodkin and Jacob Strouts are all on the bench and some others in the squad are not even here. It feels a long way away from the days we only had a couple of subs. Their keeper is struggling with his kit; it seems his shorts are too small. He tells us they didn't have a larger size and he struggles all afternoon but seems a nice lad and has a laugh about it.

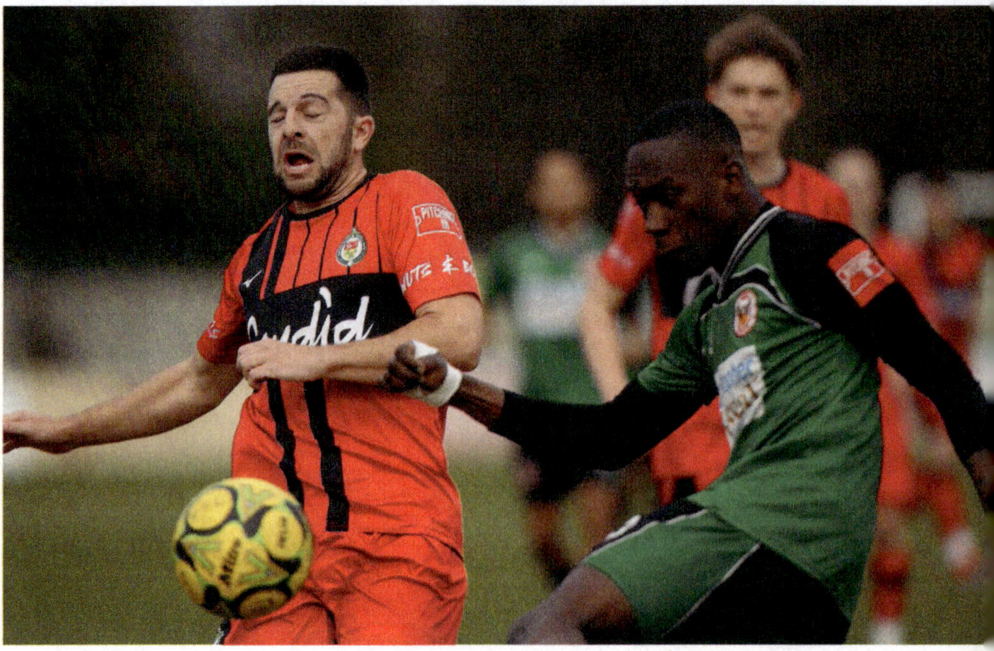

83

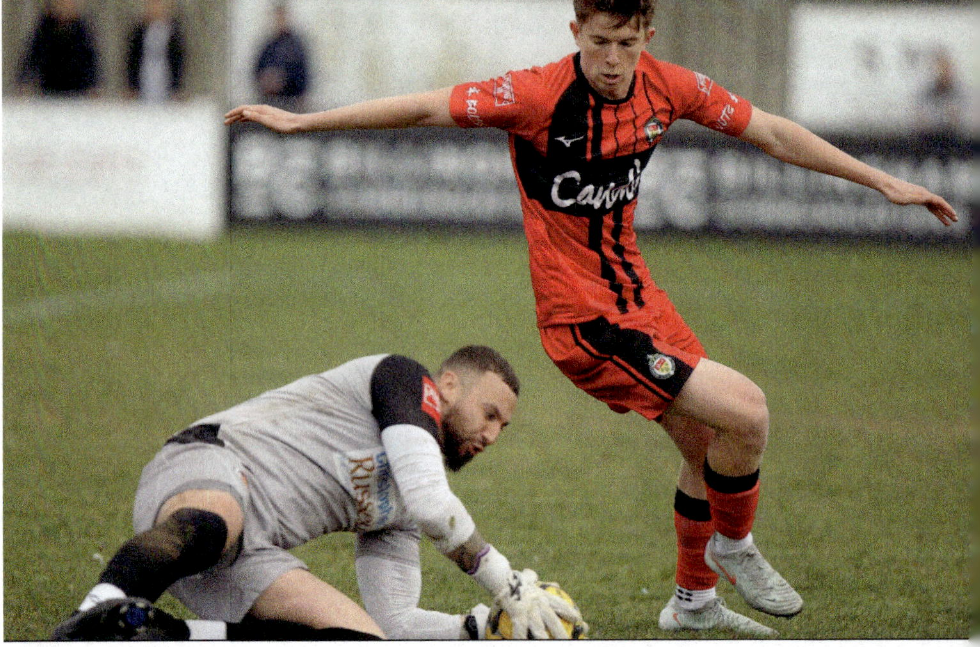

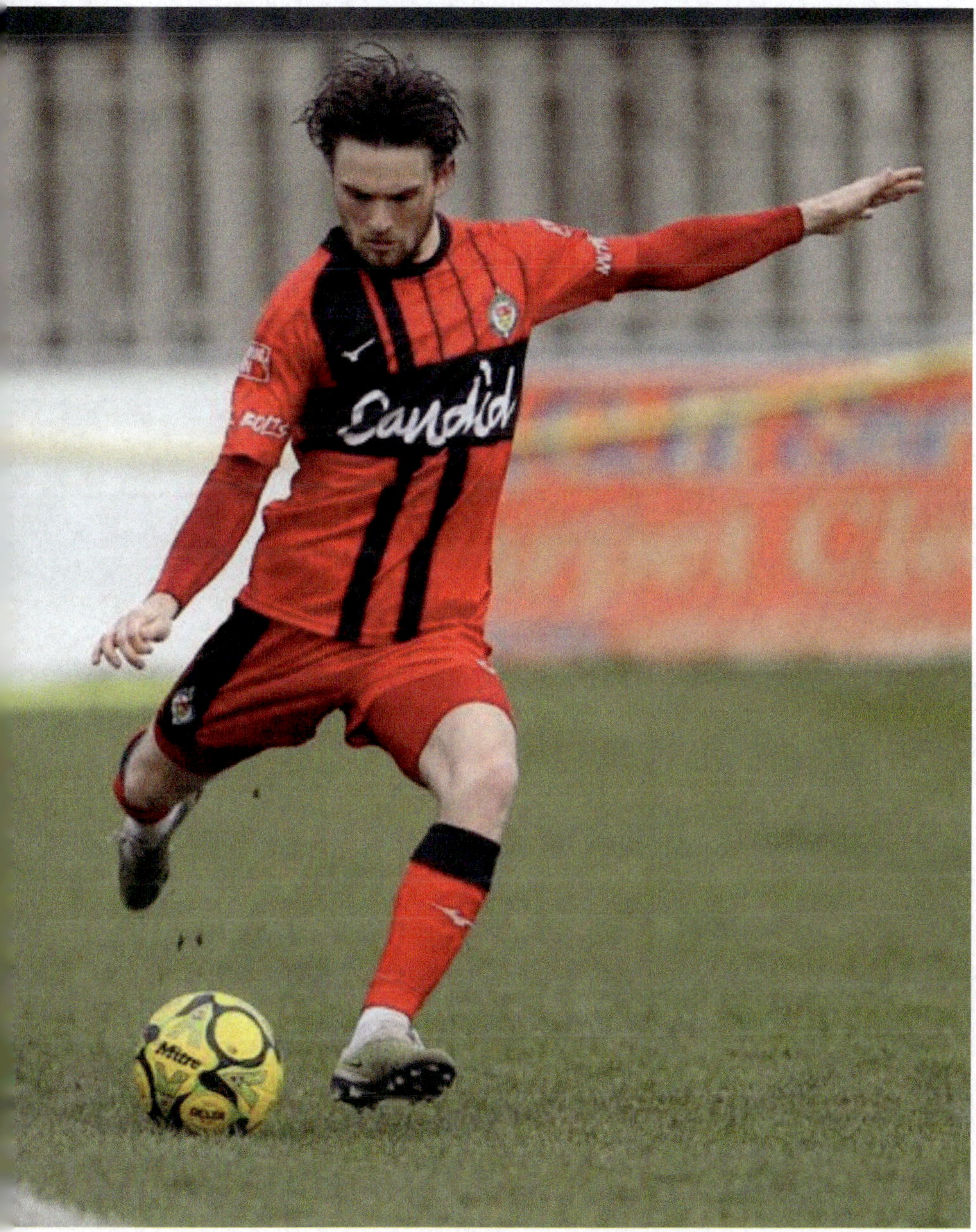
Candid
Mitre

First half is a bit messy to be honest; it seems difficult to get the ball under control on such a bumpy surface. We seem to be the better side early on although it's clear they intend to scrap this one out. Gary and Westie go close but as the half goes on Phoenix start to press and a great strike from their splendidly named striker Jerson Dos Santos and we go into the break a goal down. Surely the mystical supernatural powers or whatever they've been using against u won't prevail again. It's not for the want of trying, we know that but where's our quality today?

59th minute and yes, all our fight and hard work has paid off at last and the excellent Kane Penn is rewarded for all his hard work from right back with an excellent finish into the top corner. We're on our way, there can only be one winner, come on you……. Oh hang on, Mr Dos Santos has scored again pretty much from the restart. This is powerful sorcery they must be using! We keep fighting on, as do they and we're pressing for another equaliser. A great run and cross pass from Louis puts it on a plate for Gary who hits home and is keen to retrieve the ball from the net so we can go and get that winner. Westie is denied by Will Moses twice as he lies on the floor in the penalty box and there are half chances we don't take. Good to see Noah Carney and Will Dupray back in action and they're doing well but the third goal just doesn't come and we have to settle for the draw.

Our young 'Ultras' have banged their drum all the way through the game and there has to be as many Ashford fans here as Phoenix supporters. When we start winning things we'll have loads more but we do alright anyway and the players appreciate it.

The drive home isn't too bad. We didn't lose this one and when we beat Littlehampton in a few weeks time maybe that point will keep them up. We play a game trying to list all the teams in our league without looking them up. We fail and only get 21 teams. Eastbourne is forgettable though isn't it. Home to Sevenoaks next and Marcel's side won't be a pushover. We can't wait and let's keep the unbeaten run going COYNAB.

THREE BRIDGES

It's a bit of a drive to Crawley on a Saturday for this one and the new electric motor (Florence) is yet to be really tested with longer trips and 4 passengers (large ones). Range anxiety isn't quite surfacing and we start with a 100% charge so we'll see how we get on.

We have 2 reserve tourists in the car today with end of season excuses being made before the trip from regulars. Three Bridges still have an outside chance of the playoffs and have certainly been playing better since having to play their 'home' games at Chatham recently whilst a new pitch was being put down. We don't have good memories of previous trips to Three Bridges (always seems to rain, always don't do well and never any atmosphere or home support). The chant at the reverse fixture at the Green Box earlier in the season 'you've got more Bridges than fans' whilst cruel, isn't too far off the mark sadly. Three Bridges will blame it on being part of Crawley however how do these clubs survive with such little support? Maybe today will be different and the sunny weather certainly is a welcome change and might bring out the masses

On arrival we're met as we drive in with smiles and helpful Three Bridges staff who sell us our tickets and programmes (obvious place to sell the programme when you go in probably). Wow, this place has been given some tender loving care and not just the pitch. The place has been transformed and all the better for it.

We're early as usual and try the burgers (£6 for a double cheeseburger 8/10) and all the staff seem to have smiles on their faces and are very welcoming. We're warming up and our squad

...ks very strong again and if we can't play decent football on this surface there's something ...ong. Even the planes taking off from nearby Gatwick airport seem to be banking towards us ...get a better view of such a beautiful looking pitch.

...'re playing in red today and we can't name one of the players in the squad that we think ...n't be involved next season.

...t half and we're downwind as we kick off. Their keeper is having a nightmare dealing with ... wind and the seeming inability to kick the ball as they try to play out from the back against ... press. Louis Collins is close to charging him down on a couple of occasions and there are ...el shouts from behind the goal encouraging their defenders to pass the ball to their keeper as ...ooks so vulnerable. They simply can't clear their lines and we're hunting down loose balls ... energy and purpose. Only one team is going to score and there it is, Kane Penn, playing in ... midfield today, takes his chance at the far post. Best 45 we've played this season? Maybe ... for all our industry and good work we didn't make too many chances. Tolu unfortunately ...n't lasted long and has gone off with a knee problem and Joey Taylor takes his place.

...'re all smiling and confident come halftime and hoping for more goals. Their striker, Noel ...ghton, is sent off for a second yellow and well deserved. Surely against 10 men we'll win this ...ily. Their manager has obviously given them a rocket at halftime and they look like a ...erent team, winning the second balls and seizing on our mistakes. The inevitable happens ... they head home an equaliser, unthinkable in the first half. There's not much noise as there ... so few home supporters here which is sad for them. Suddenly we start wondering if we're ...g to lose, what's going on!. Joey has had to go off and Will Dupray is on which means Kane ... gone back to full back. We're looking tired and only manage one real chance as the game ...rs 90 minutes; Gary's header saved well by their keeper. It's lovely to see Tolu and Joey ...ing with fans behind the goal as no longer involved on the pitch.

That sort of thing makes some kids weekends.

We take a draw and 5 unbeaten and start the drive home. We're all very disappointed which weird as I'm sure we'd have been happy with an away draw with a team several places above us in the table before we left home. There's discussions about learnings Lloyd will take from today, blacmanges (had to be there) and Operation Brock or whatever they call it now. One temporary tourist helpfully pointed out on the way to the match, on the M23 near Gatwick, that they were putting Brock up for Easter so if we were driving to Littlehampton we'd need to bear that in mind. It had to be pointed out that was why we were driving at 50mph for half an hour earlier on the M20 as it was already there! He hadn't noticed and maybe because there was

single lorry queuing. Maybe they'll be a few on the way back because surely the authorities
ve thought through the necessity of imposing M20 hassle on everyone, again! Nope, not a
gle one as we reach Ashford in good time despite the speed restrictions.

ice sunny day, a game we were going to easily win that ultimately was a disappointment,
wever the good news was that Florence was reporting that she still had 53% battery when we
home; not bad, not bad at all.
rely we can beat relegated Steyning Town next weekend at the Green Box; we shall see
YNAB!

TLEHAMPTON TOWN

aven forbid you'd ever be found doing anything constructive" were the harsh words one
rist was trying to process as he sought refuge on the long drive to Littlehampton. It was bad
ugh that he was still recovering from last week's aberration at the Green Box against
yning Town but now he had to deal with this marital rebuke and just because he'd forgotten
now the lawn, as instructed, having become transfixed with a Laurel and Hardy box set.
metimes life is tough. It's well over 200 miles this round trip but we have every confidence in
rence and her battery capacity; we don't want to be recharging on the way home.

ehampton has never been a destination venue for us but as we get there the old, dilapidated
den stand has gone, replaced by a metal one that's OK. Other than that and the fact that
r unruly yobs that used to attach themselves to the club seem to have gone, nothing much
 has changed. It's the start of the cricket season and on the cricket side of the temporary
ce they've prepared a decent looking square and outfield however on the football pitch side
pretty poor with end of season grass scarcity on show. Hopefully nobody gets injured playing
this today.

many Ashfordians here today understandably given the distance and how far we were off
ing any decent football last weekend. There are a few and a drum and we'll do our best to
er the lads on.

Although the unexpected rain is unpleasant it probably does the game some good as it settles the mud and grass pitch down somewhat and the bounce of the ball is dampened down a touch. We already look like a different side to last week. We're closing down, fighting for the ball with energy and determination. Harrison Pont is playing centre back with Will Moses out injured and looks assured as does the other Harrison, Harrison Hume who's assured touch and energy in midfield (he's in for the injured Joey Taylor) is pleasing on the eye. Gary is in a rich vein of form and he's scored twice and is now just 5 away from the all time Ashford scoring record. At half time we deserve our two goal lead; that was a good half.

The staff at Littlehampton are friendly enough. The burgers are ok (7/10 and £5 for a bacon burger) but we fall for the old full price Mars Bar ploy for Action Man sized confectionery; still needs must on a cool and miserable afternoon.

For the first time in the game Littlehampton push us back and we lose control of the game for 10 minutes. They score from a set piece but hopefully we'll manage the game better today especially as Lloyd has been drilling into the players at every opportunity how important game management is. We gradually regain control and start to break dangerously. Louis Collins never stops running and deserves his well taken goal that puts this one to bed. Littlehampton fight manfully in a meaningless game for them and their numbers 2 and 15 impress however we are the better side by a distance today. It's a shame young Archie McCarthy (coming on for his second game as sub for us today) doesn't connect properly when he breaks and doesn't trouble the keeper but it's great to see Gary and the management team clap him and encourage rather than moan.

The long drive home is interrupted by a call from Redders at Radio Ashford wanting to know about the game. Ashford is treated to a couple of songs from today's tourists on live radio and although we probably sounded inebriated no alcohol was consumed by anyone on board; we were probably just a bit drunk on success at last (easily pleased it could be argued!).

We're looking forward to Easter Monday at the Green Box against Hythe now, what could go wrong? When we finally get back to Ashford it's probably still light enough for lawn mowing and Florence exceeded all expectations and still had 33% battery; pretty, pretty good! COYNAB.

MARGATE

10th August 2024 and the league started with a thrilling 3-3 draw away at newly promoted Erith Town. The final match of this season's campaign is, on paper, a pretty meaningless game away at Margate. They will want to maintain momentum prior to their big playoff semi final game on Tuesday away at Burgess Hill. It's not meaningless to Lloyd or the players however and it's certainly not meaningless to today's tourists; we want a good performance today against a good side. We're envious of the teams in the playoffs but we're a good side and last Easter Monday we scored some great goals back at the Green Box and we want more entertainment like that it's not too much to ask for.

This was the first trip to Hartsdown Park for the majority of us today and we're expecting a nice stadium given the time they spent in higher leagues. We find the place a bit of a disappointment if we're honest with two sides of the ground empty. The pitch looks to be a good surface but that's about all and again we're thankful to have a home like the Green Box.

s is Thanet and whilst we left Ashford in warm sunshine it's rarely warm here with an easterly
ing. A wardrobe miscalculation has left one tourist, the silly boy, shivering in a tee shirt and
rts. It will be a long afternoon for him.

to get in here and concessions £8 which is a bit high so we're very grateful to Lloyd for
ing the entrance to everyone who went to Littlehampton (nice gesture that). It's £5 for a
ger (6/10) and the chips are said to be good but apparently being served at all was a long
wn out affair. No Mars Bars or anything available at the tea bar which is disappointing but
ably a good thing after all the Easter chocolate consumed of late. A decent enough crowd
e and it's good to have a quick chat with Adam Flanagan (Margate Assistant Manager) and
 him well for Tuesday. Also good to see Harvey Brand and Max Walsh; we liked them when
 played for us.

Gary get closer to the record today? If he gets a hat trick that would do it and whilst we
ldn't put it past him this lot beat Ramsgate away 4-1 last week and are certainly no mugs.

You wouldn't know who the team is in the playoffs though from the way we're playing in the fir half; it's all Ashford but, for once, our finishing is off. We create several good chances but it's r going in. We're looking assured at the back as well. All good fun but at the end of the half it looks like another ex Ashford player Lewis Knight picks up what looks like a nasty injury which delays things. Hopefully he'll be OK for the playoffs but it looks unlikely.

It's obvious there's good support for Ashford which is great to see and we're hopeful to get something today out of the game as we change ends. They start off slightly the better and pus us back and unfortunately we go behind on the hour; that's a shame. We fight back, push forward and again create some great chances. They clear off the line from a Gary header anc Westie can't make good contact from close range. It doesn't look to be our day despite being the better team. Barry Fuller is pushed in the box and we are given a penalty. Gary's missed few this season but takes responsibility. It's not a good penalty and it's saved well. This isn't c day. When the final whistle comes we're not down hearted at a 1-0 defeat. We've played well with good energy and spirit and it bodes well for next season.

All the away support gather straight after the game to applaud their team and thank them for their efforts this season. Lloyd makes an impromptu speech announcing the Players Player o the season as voted for by the fans. Louis Collins picks up the well deserved award and has beaming smile on his face.

y Lockyer is voted Players Player of the season and is confirmed as club captain for next son; well deserved.

We head off home and one tourist asks Florence to defrost him; he won't make the mistake of going to an April game on the Isle of Thanet again under dressed! It's been the usual ups and downs and we reflect on the best and the worst of the year, the most enjoyable and the most depressing. It's been good fun and although we're all looking forward to a few weekends off we all can't wait to get started again. Are the first friendly pre-season games at the end of June? When will training start? Will we be hearing of any new signings sooner or later? We contemplate on what we're going to do with ourselves for the next couple of months but it won't be long before four men and a car will be off on tour around the south of England again and we're looking forward to it!

Thanks to Nick Watson, Kenny Sharpe, Dave Jones, Ian Scammell, Phil Richardson and Andrew Woolnough for all their help along the way.

Photos by Jez Holme, Dave Jones and Nick Watson. Any decent photos probably taken by Oyster Bay Photography (Ian Scammell).

Copyright J Holme 2025 "all rights reserved"

Printed in Dunstable, United Kingdom